Boo

HOLIDAY CRUISING
IN FRANCE

The 'Holiday Cruising' series

HOLIDAY CRUISING ON INLAND WATERWAYS
by Charles Hadfield and Michael Streat

HOLIDAY CRUISING ON THE THAMES
by E. and P. W. Ball

HOLIDAY CRUISING ON THE BROADS AND FENS
by Lewis Edwards

HOLIDAY CRUISING IN IRELAND
by P. J. G. Ransom

HOLIDAY CRUISING IN FRANCE
by Gerard Morgan-Grenville

Other books by Gerard Morgan-Grenville

BARGING INTO FRANCE
BARGING INTO SOUTHERN FRANCE

in preparation

NAVIGATOR'S GUIDE TO THE FRENCH INLAND WATERWAYS

HOLIDAY CRUISING
IN FRANCE

GERARD MORGAN-GRENVILLE

with plates, text illustrations and map

DAVID & CHARLES: NEWTON ABBOT

ISBN 0 7153 5829 4

To all who seek to preserve and improve our environment

Set in 11 pt Times New Roman 2 pt leaded
and printed in Great Britain
by Latimer Trend & Company Limited Plymouth
for David & Charles (Holdings) Limited
South Devon House Newton Abbot Devon

Contents

Contents

List of Illustrations

List of Illustrations

The photographs are by the author, with the exception of: 'One of the last electric traction "horses", now defunct' supplied by Studio Rogers, 57 rue St-Jean, 57-Nancy, France; 'The *Palinurus* hotel boat' supplied by Continental Waterway Cruises Ltd, 21 Hans Place SW1; and 'A hire cruiser on the Nivernais' and 'Reflections in the Yonne' supplied by Saint Line Cruisers, La Montagne, La Collancelle, 58-Corbigny, France.

The cover photograph is supplied by Peter Zivy of Saint Line Cruisers.

Introduction

As you push off from the quay at the start of your journey, whether in the simplicity of a canoe or the luxury of a well-fitted motor cruiser, you are about to enjoy an experience which will probably rank amongst the happiest of your life.

You are entering another world, a world in which you are truly the master of your fate. The daily punctuations of meal and sleep are yours to place as you will; it is for you to dictate the tempo of your own life as you please. The daily cares recede into that other world where clock and duty lay claim to your waking day. You can relax, you *will* relax. It is hopeless to resist!

You are heading into a life amongst a friendly people who will respect you for what you are—someone who obviously wants to see France as it *really* is. You are not just another faceless English tourist screeching southward along the motorway bound for the Mediterranean beaches. You are someone who has chosen to explore an area of France and to become—temporarily—a part of it.

For this reason, I think, you will find people kindly disposed toward you. It would be stupid to endanger this happy relationship by causing needless irritation to your hosts and, since it is possible to do this quite unwittingly, you should learn the Rules of the Game. For the rest, commonsense and ordinary good manners will be your guide.

And here you have not only yourself to consider, for after

you will be others. Put another way, the natural goodwill you encounter has not been jeopardised by those before you.

The French do not exploit their canals and rivers as cruising grounds. Indeed, there are very few leisure craft of the type one sees moored along every mile of British inland waterway. Occasionally, though, you do see a smooth-faced young man from Paris tearing up an otherwise quiet stretch of river in a motor boat fitted with a pointlessly powerful engine, trying to impress a bikini-clad girl with the connotations of power and speed. And occasionally too, you see something like a floating bedroom moored within reach of one of the larger cities. But the idea of a holiday spent aboard a small craft winding its way across whole *départements* is not treated seriously, at least not at present. Lack of initiative or lack of appreciation for an amenity as yet unthreatened? A study of the French mentality in the light of this curious neglect is, I fear, a digression which will not be tolerated! But there it is— some of the most peaceful cruising grounds in Europe are yours to explore—and *explore* is not always too strong a word!

If the French do not value their waterways for pleasure cruising, they more than make up for the omission by utilising every metre of bank as a fishing-base. No *Anglais* can readily appreciate the fanatical reverence the average Frenchman feels for his national pastime. To this fishing fraternity, the waterways are imaginary stewponds teeming with every species of fish. A passing barge, churning up the mud along a canal, may ruin the fishing for a considerable period. Consequently, *pêcheurs* and *mariniers* are traditional enemies.

Fishing is a force in local politics and there have been concerted attempts to close certain little-used canals in order to leave the fishing undisturbed. An appreciation of this balance of interests between the two waterway users is fundamental to a successful holiday.

The only aquatic activities to have caught the imagination of the French—so far as the rivers are concerned—are dinghy sailing and water skiing. These sports are normally practised in short, clearly signed stretches of river, generally a few kilometres from the larger towns.

For the remaining 99 per cent of the available water area, the canals and canalised rivers can be fairly readily divided into those used heavily by commercial craft and those which see only occasional use and as a result are threatened with closure. With ruthless and self-defeating logic, the French authorities allocate money for waterway maintenance according to the tonnage which uses each section. Since a canal costs the same whether it is used little or often, to give less money to a seldom-used waterway is to condemn it to a slow death from weed, erosion and decay. If a greater use can be made of these 'redundant' waterways and their lives prolonged, I feel justified in advertising the idea of holiday cruising in France. It so happens that all of these little-used waterways are ideal for the purpose and all are beautiful. The same cannot always be said of the busier routes. (In the section devoted to the individual routes I have indicated the amount of traffic likely to be encountered.)

My sincere hope is that I may encourage the use of these slowly decaying water-roads, so that their future may be assured. My candid fear is that, instead of being used, they may be abused.

In my experience, misuse most often derives from ignorance or thoughtlessness, rather than design. Please do not think me patronising if you find the observations which follow rather obvious. If you do, let me assure you that I have occasionally seen fellow-countrymen act in direct contravention of these golden rules.

It is not an exaggeration to say that maltreatment of a canal or outrageous behaviour could decisively militate against the future of the waterway. It does not take much imagination to foresee, for example, that if you discharge a gallon of sump oil into a canal, an important surface area of water will be contaminated. This will harm or kill the fish and obviously it will give the outraged fishermen some powerful ammunition to fire in the appropriate direction. If he has also suffered wet feet because your excessive wash inundated his fishing platform, he will be even less pleased. Such behaviour scarcely helps promote the *entente cordiale*. So now for Four Golden Rules. I mention these now not only in case you fail to read on (where you will find them enlarged upon) but in the hope that, above all else, these few points will remain constantly in the front of your mind.

NEVER jettison into the water any pollutant or imperishable.

NEVER set up a wash which erodes the bank.

NEVER overtake a commercial barge within a mile of a lock —the livelihood of the crew depends on timely arrival at their destination.

BEHAVE with extra courtesy towards all whom you meet, especially the fishermen and those engaged in the service of the waterways.

Burgate House   G.M.-G.
Godalming
Surrey   September 1972

CHAPTER ONE

Why France?

I address this book to all who wish to explore the water-ways of France. There are many countries whose maps show a network of rivers and canals but none, with the possible exception of Russia, can provide the inland navigator with such a rich variety of scenery or climate. And what country can hope to compete with the dazzling diversity of architecture or kitchen? You do not need to be a student of history or a Master of Wine to experience the felicity of mind and tongue which each day's travel brings.

The waterways of France are a world of their own and exert a powerful magic which will bind you for life. They are travelled by an itinerant nation of hardworking bargee families. Their vast fleet is complemented by an assortment of other craft, from tugs and dredgers to what must surely rank as the world's largest flotilla of fishing punts.

The bargees, whose world this is, maintain a strong family tradition within their profession and it is by no means rare to find fifth- or sixth-generation mariners. Nomadic and independent, they constitute a race apart, bound firmly to one another by shared skills, a shared history, shared hardships and rewards and, above all, by a passionate attachment to their chosen way of life. They ply an ancient trade, yet one which has kept pace with the demands of a changing environment. They probably work as hard as anyone—a seven-day week, rising before dawn and continuing until darkness is complete. They are used to sudden and sometimes prolonged poverty when work is scarce. Yet they maintain their craft with impeccable cleanliness within and without. They manoeuvre their unwieldy barges with the skill of virtuosos and, with astonishingly few exceptions, show the foreigner a courtesy which is humbling.

France has some five thousand miles of maintained water-way—two and a half times the English mileage—and the standard of maintenance is extraordinarily high. The locks and moving bridges are all manned. Advised by telephone of your impending arrival, it is normal to find the next lock set ready to receive you. Queueing is rare in comparison to the English, Belgian or Dutch waterways. Facilities such as water points and fuel pumps are located in convenient quay-side positions.

'This is all very well,' you may say, with British realism, 'but conditions such as these need paying for and, besides, there is an awkward language problem. Splendid for the fortunate few with a good supply of francs in the pocket and *mots francais* on the tongue! But the humble British holiday-cruise enthusiast is better off in Britain!'

Is he?

How much for a licence to cruise the French waterways? Nothing. How much to pass through the locks? Nothing. How much for a mooring? Nothing. How much to fill the tanks with water? Nothing. *Gratuit, Monsieur,* and you are very welcome! Just how welcome you will not know until you can experience it for yourself.

And the language? Well, it is true that English is not the *lingua franca* of the French waterways. And let us assume that you know nothing of the French language. In the first place you won't need to say very much—if you don't want to. The requirements of a man in a boat are fairly self-evident: If you throw a line to someone on a quay and point at a bollard you'll be surprised how quickly and willingly some kind of knot is applied. The French are not stupid! Nor are they unhelpful. When you need a new sparking-plug or a loaf

14

of bread, you may be amazed how a single word suffices to indicate the location of a source. And if you don't like to chance your accent you can always point to the word in a dictionary or a phrase book. (As these sometimes have the depressing characteristic of listing every word or phrase except the one you want, a specialised glossary is included at the end of this book.)

I cannot believe that language is any barrier to a boatman. You would not be a cruising enthusiast were you not independent and imaginative. The same qualities, aided by uninhibited gesticulation, will suffice to make you self-reliant. I have often met English crews without a word of French between them.

The waterways offer all conditions. You can compete in the wide rivers with vessels of several thousand tons or you can range one of the quiet canals where you may not encounter another craft for an entire day. You can travel in luxury in a hotel boat or paddle a kayak. You can cross upland plateaux a thousand or more feet above sea level or cruise a tranquil valley far beneath the hills and rocky peaks. You can moor under the ancient quays of Paris or drift through antiquated villages where fairy-tale castles stand unchanged by the passage of time. The choice is yours.

Everywhere you will encounter friendliness and hospitality. You will feast yourself on the scenery and gorge yourself with the most succulent meals. For if you are doing your own cooking you will find new materials of a quality hardly known in Britain; wine for a few pence a bottle.

I'm not sure that everyone encountered in a boat is there for the same reason. Some want to press on and cover great distances, some to potter and yet others are content just to scrape, paint and polish. But one thing is predictable. Whatever motivates you, you will be captivated by navigating your chosen corner of France, even if your 'navigation' hardly moves. You will start an endless honeymoon with the slowly curving waterways, the beguiling beauty of an unspoilt land-

15

scape, as varied as any in Europe; fields resplendent with flowers the long summer through; the slow tempo of people not yet convinced of the merits of 'progress' at any price. If I wax euphoric, you cannot blame me: the honeymoon is still with me even after many years and the ups and downs of a thousand or more locks.

BACKGROUND TO THE WATERWAYS NETWORK

On the premise that the interest of those who read this book originated with our own English canals, I feel it appropriate to start by comparing the development of the canal and river systems of England and France.

In many ways the development ran parallel. The purpose of the operation in each case was to facilitate the carriage of people and the transport of goods. In pre-Roman days, the main channels of communication in France, as in England, were the navigable rivers. These were the land's natural arteries. It therefore followed that almost all the earliest settlements hugged these rivers, and it was not until the need to join together the developing centres made itself felt that an interconnecting canal system became highly desirable.

Even on the rivers themselves the limitations of horse-drawn haulage and the hazards, or impossibility, of navigating upstream, meant that many centuries were needed to tame these rivers and develop anything like regular transport systems from them.

The roads were often impassable, especially in winter. Even in England as recently as 150 years ago it could take at least two days to travel the 115 miles from London to Bristol and similar delays were common in France, in spite of a road system which was vastly superior to its English counterpart. So, with railways as yet undreamed of, the development of the waterway systems was an entirely logical progression.

Whereas the great canal-building mania swept across England towards the end of the eighteenth century, in France

Page 17 (*left*) A typical lifting bridge; (*right*) a typical Freycinet standard lock

Page 18 (*above*) The barge is equally close to the other side of the lock; (*below*) emerging from the tunnel of Foug, under traction

there was considerable development more than a hundred years earlier. The systems employed in England for canal building, changing levels, tunnelling and so on were generally similar in concept to those already in use in France.

But this is where the parallel between the two systems ends. For an appreciation of subsequent evolution the main differences must be understood. They stem mainly from a divergence of outlook which continues to the present day. The British canals were originally mainly private ventures. In France, the State was usually the patron, with the result that from the earliest days the greater tendency towards standardisation was to be found in France. Because of France's greater size and the increased distances over which goods had to be moved—to say nothing of the French passion for doing things in the grand manner—France developed its waterways on a far larger scale than did England. This increased scale extended to the vessels employed on canals and when, in 1879, the government laid down the generous Freycinet standard lock dimensions of 126ft by 17ft 3in, the viability of the French waterways up to the present time was largely assured. This, in spite of the great parallel growth of railways, which was steadily rendering the English network of smaller waterways unprofitable. So that today the most obvious difference in the two systems is that, whilst the one is largely a relic of a waterway system which, through lack of foresight and co-ordination, fell into disuse, the other is still a vigorous enterprise, an integral and major part of the country's network of communications. The figures speak for themselves. In 1900 the inland fleet carried 32 million tons; by 1960 the tonnage had increased to 68 million and the figure for 1970 is no less than 110 million tons. But this is not to say that France lacks examples of waterways which proved unprofitable and were abandoned because they were too small (like the *Canal du Berry*) or of canalised rivers which led nowhere of adequate commercial importance (the Eure, for example) or many of the other waterways which are in imminent danger of being 'suppressed' (such as the Mayenne, Sarthe, Charente, Seille, *Canal du Bourgogne*, to name but a few).

As for practical differences, the French have enjoyed a slight advantage over the English in that, over the whole canal system, France's average gradient is 3·51ft per mile, as against the British average of 4·09ft per mile. But this apparent favouritism on the part of nature is cancelled out by France's less abundant water with which to work the canals and the substantially greater engineering work needed to ensure adequate supply.

Consequently, apart from their visibly flourishing state, probably the feature which will most impress the English traveller visiting the French waterways is the massive—I was tempted to say *permanent*—nature of the 'works'. The French inherited the Roman genius for civil engineering and nowhere is this more evident than in the beautifully built structures which still stand almost exactly as they were built—some as far back as 1605.

I can hear the English canal enthusiast hurling abuse at me for implying that the English canal system is the poor relation. But in structure, size and success it cannot compare. In spite of this, I would willingly agree that the history of British waterways is no less interesting and that their future— if bleak at present—should indeed be as golden as that of their cross-Channel cousins. And this leads me to a minor but relevant digression.

If, as I hope, you share my view that canals and canalised rivers ought primarily to serve the interests for which they were designed—those of freight transportation—and only incidentally to provide scope for the waterborne summer wanderer, then your visit to the waterways of France will utterly convince you. We, the long-suffering British public, are quite needlessly being burdened with a road transport headache that successive governments have cared ludicrously little to alleviate.

Why France?

Have you, as you drove behind the bulk of a slow-moving long-distance lorry, paused to consider why it is there at all? Have you, as you coughed your way past the black cloud of diesel fumes, stopped to consider that goods trains nowadays seem a rarity, that barges seem an anachronism? If you have, then go to France and have your suspicions confirmed. For you will see the bulk carriage of goods being handled by those traditional enemies, the barge and the rail-wagon. The inland fleet of France carries loads that would require some *twenty million* lorry journeys to transport—and the majority of trains are freight-carrying.

When we have a greater success in forcing ourselves and our politicians into realising responsibilities to the quality of life as distinct from material prosperity, and when our planners have understood the Grand Concept of Inland Navigation, then, and only then, may we expect to see reduced the ever-growing menace of blocked roads, casualties caused by frustrated drivers, noise and the poisonous effects of exhaust. But waterway redevelopment will only follow in the wake of informed public opinion. So, when you are convinced, as you will surely be, you will be serving the interests of your fellow-beings by becoming vociferous.

Like most man-made waterway systems the French canals have been dug to connect rivers whose waters are derived from opposing basins or catchment areas. A glance at the map will show that the two major river complexes, the Seine and Rhône–Saône, embrace some of the most important (and most attractive) link canals. In the more heavily industrialised north-eastern quarter of France, this Seine to Rhône network is itself linked to several other major rivers, none wholly French, such as the Lys, Escaut, Sambre and Meuse, which all flow north-east into Belgium, and the Moselle which disappears northwards across the French boundary into Germany: the Rhine itself forming the frontier between France and Germany.

The third great river complex of France—after the Seine

21

and the Rhône—is the Loire, a fallen giant of French interior navigation. Almost all that is left of this group of waterways are the canals and canalised rivers of Brittany, an area rich in cruising possibilities but largely bereft of commercial navigation.

Lastly (apart from a few more or less unconnected canalised rivers on the west coast) the famous link-canal *du Midi* joins the Garonne on the Atlantic coast to the Mediterranean.

This then is the main grouping of the canal and river regions. Each has its own peculiar characteristics both in the execution of the 'works' and in the design of the craft used—though this is now generally apparent only with the older barges constructed forty or more years ago. Many of these are still to be seen in varying stages of disrepair and their diversity forms a fascinating study, for there are some seventy distinct branches in the family tree of the French inland cargo-carrying vessel.

When considering the variety, construction and volume of traffic, one has to remember that France is three times the size of Britain, that conditions of wind, flood and river current are all more extreme than anything encountered by the British bargee. The Rhône, for example, has current speeds of up to 10 knots and can have wind speeds of over 100mph. The Loire has a water flow variation factor of over 100:1 representing an autumn depth in many places of a scant six inches. Yet, in spite of these and numerous other hazards, the importance of the rivers as the only feasible agent of commercial transport was such that, at the height of its navigational use, on the Loire alone 4,000 boats made a one-way descent of the river in a single year. In one Loire riverside town some 600 carpenters were permanently employed in making the craft which were broken up on arrival at their destination.

The different areas of the network of waterways comprised a great variety of haulage systems and their study is also an absorbing subject.

Why France?

I hope that this brief introduction will provide a foundation on which the observant traveller can start to build a picture of the bygone age in which this vast water roadway was constructed.

CHAPTER TWO

Preparations

METHODS OF CRUISING

The word *cruise* seems to imply deck-chairs filled with sun-bronzed bodies, a blazing sun and a white-coated steward hurrying forward with a tray of iced drinks! Certainly it is difficult to escape connotations of luxury and idleness. So perhaps I should start by making it clear that the kind of cruising that concerns us here allows the broadest interpretation of the word. At one extremity the first image is accurate enough; at the other we touch, if but briefly, on the humbler paddle-it-yourself canoe. For what we are really concerned with is the exploration of the French waterways. Our means of travel is of secondary importance.

Starting with the least energetic (and consequently the most expensive) there are a few rivers, like the Seine, Rhône and Charente, which can be explored on the basis of day-cruises, followed by nights at hotels. Since this way of travel is confined to very few areas, and since the cruises are of short duration it would, I think, be difficult to put together a reasonable itinerary likely to give much satisfaction to someone with limited time and resources. It would be better to avail oneself of these opportunities *en passant* on a car-based journey. A list of such services is given in Appendix C.

The next method, which comes a great deal closer to the heart of the matter, is to utilise one of the hotel boats. These offer the traveller a chance of a more intimate relationship

24

with the waterway and its custodians, and the smaller the ship the more this is true. For those who cannot, for one reason or another, think in terms of propelling themselves in a boat, these services may offer the best alternative. The boats are not luxurious by the standards of Caribbean cruisers but one's reasonable requirements are amply catered for and the cost is very fair. Appendix C lists the few possibilities at present available.

Now we come to the hire cruiser. The options are wider here, though seen in the context of the whole waterway network, the cruising grounds are still limited. But there is a real choice of scenery and climate and there are many alternatives of boat.

The great advantage of this method is that you are freed from any kind of organisational worry. Furthermore, the hirer provides for virtually all contingencies: you are most unlikely to be at a disadvantage—other than briefly—even if you do have a flat battery or a broken propeller. For a *single* journey it could be cheaper than taking your own boat to the same place. In hiring such a cruiser you may well be able to afford a more luxurious boat than you could own. Everything is provided: all you have to do is to turn up at the right place at the appointed time. If you are worried as to whether you will 'manage' a motor cruiser—or even as to whether you will like the life—this must be the way to start.

Hiring out motor cruisers is not an easy way of making money (I have tried!) and the charges are extremely reasonable in relation to the craft and service offered. Again, Appendix C lists the services available.

Now we come to the best means of all of travelling through France: in your own boat. I have devoted a separate short section to the question of choosing a boat so I will now confine myself to praising the method. For extensive journeying it is certainly the cheapest. You have complete flexibility of itinerary—the whole of the 5,000 miles of river and canal system is yours to explore. You will start (if you have not already done so) an emotional involvement with boat and waterway which will put you amongst the most fortunate of humans.

Finally, there is the canoe or kayak. (I suppose there is also the rowable dinghy, but having rowed down a long part of the Loire, I cannot recommend this life, undoubtedly healthy though it is!) But with a craft as streamlined and as light as a modern canoe or kayak, you can make excellent progress. The advantages here are that virtually all the rivers of France are open to you—a total distance which would take years to paddle. Navigation in canoe or kayak is unrestricted: no authorisation is required and there are no special regulations governing the use of locks or weirs. Providing you are prepared to live simply you can take your tent and cooker and there can be no cheaper life. Or you can travel like Robert Louis Stevenson, who first introduced British readers to the joys of French rivers and canals in *An Inland Voyage*; travelling by canoe with a friend he moved from waterside hotel to waterside hotel.

Canoe–kayak travellers are well catered for in France. Excellent maps and information sheets are obtainable from the Touring Club of France and a book listed in Appendix H 'Maps and Publications' gives a brief synopsis of all the canoeable rivers and canals. My only advice to canoeists is to avoid the double variety if you wish to remain on speaking terms with your partner. Canoeing is not for you if you are immoderately depressed at the prospect of capsizing.

CHOOSING A CRUISER

I plan to be a little circumspect in making judgements under this heading. For one reason or another most people do not have complete freedom of choice when it comes to buying a boat—any more than they do in house purchase.

In fact, in making a purchase, a boat is not unlike a house:

if the hull and deck (walls and roof) are in good condition, it does not really matter too much about the rest. You may even consider it an advantage that the interior is a mess, for the price will be lower and the job of fitting *can* be the greatest fun.

I shall not attempt to guide you through the boatyards of Britain or France. Suffice it to say that there are good and bad boats and both honest and diabolical dealers. As in all business transactions it makes sense to deal with an organisation with a good reputation to maintain. Most boat owners believe their craft to be better than it actually is. So if you are not conversant with the know-how of boat assessment my firm advice is, leave it to someone who is. Do not buy the first boat you see even if you like it and 'there is someone else interested'. There are plenty more! Shopping around for boats need not be too difficult as most yards are open at weekends and on summer evenings.

Age

Age is a consideration. There are fine old boats, in excellent condition, offering solid comfort and pleasing lines. They can be a better purchase than newer craft. Just because a boat is aged it is not necessarily fit for the breakers' yard. My own boat has a sixty-year-old iron hull—and it is still thicker and stronger than those of similar boats built of inferior steel this year. And because it was so old, it was very cheap.

Type and Size

I have never known anyone who, financial considerations apart, wanted a craft *smaller* than the one he was in, so I think it fair to say 'buy as large as you can afford'. But condition comes in here; and I mean *condition* rather than *age*. For if you buy cheaply a large boat in poor condition, you may find that the job of putting it into repair will be disproportionately expensive.

Apart from your pocket, a limiting factor can be the size of the waterway 'works'. When you consult the map section you will see the vital statistics of each canal or river. But size in France hardly imposes the restrictions that it does in England. Nonetheless, catamarans and trimarans can easily be too broad for the locks and often of too fragile a construction to make suitable waterway cruisers.

Sailing yachts may have a fixed keel too deep for the available depth. If you are buying a yacht it is a bad idea to have one whose mast exceeds the overall length of the boat. The overhang, when the mast is stepped, can very easily cause damage or be damaged when manoeuvering. (Incidentally, there is no problem in having masts stepped or even stored when entering France.) Obviously there is no point in buying a sailing yacht unless you want to sail. The accommodation, length for length or price for price, is much more restricted than in a motor cruiser. But there are *some* good craft which represent sensible compromises between the two species, if you want both to sail and to cruise.

The general rule with size is to avoid buying a craft that is on the limit of the specified dimensions; this applies more to vertical measurements than horizontal ones.

Most people prefer four-berth to two-berth boats. The latter start at around 16ft in length. It is difficult to design a satisfactory four-berth boat less than 22ft or even 24ft long, though many designs do exist. In a boat of this length you will need to be tidy and you may find yourselves rather on top of each other. If it is a boat with a wide beam it will be more roomy, but each extra foot you can add above 24ft makes for a surprising amount of additional comfort. At about 28ft some cruisers become six-berth and at around 34ft there are eight-berth models—although eight people in 34ft of boat can sometimes seem like two too many!

Beware of the terminology: 3/4, 4/6, 6/8, etc berth. Usually the first figure represents the number of berths and the second the number that can be squeezed in, using extra lilos or camp-beds, usually on the cockpit floor. My advice is to forget the second figure and to downgrade the manufacturer or salesman for using a description that can be misleading.

Prices

New motor cruisers of the 22–35ft type, in fibreglass and completely fitted out including engine, can cost between £2,000 and £10,000 and you *can* pay even more. Motor-sailers are always considerably higher in price, size for size, and most people find themselves looking at second-hand boats fairly early on in their search for anything of this size which sails well and is really seaworthy. For those who are sufficiently practical to complete the job themselves, you can buy the basic hull of many cruisers and yachts for as little as £500 for a four-berth design. But if you are not a real handyman this is *certainly* not for you.

In the second-hand or 'used' boat market £1,000 will buy you a very passable four- or even six-berth motor cruiser and indeed you could pay a lot less than this . . . which is where the expert knowledge comes in!

Narrow Boats

The width of many English canal locks is only 7ft. Consequently there are a great number of 'narrow' boats made in this country. They are *not* ideal for Continental use. In terms of volume they are poor value for money and they tend to be unsteady due to the narrow beam.

English or French?

France is not a good hunting-ground for boats. The selection is very poor. Recently the French started to make some strangely unattractive craft that resemble caravans floating on rafts. These can be a danger in a cross wind and would be useless for coastal cruising.

Perhaps the only positive advantage of buying French is in relation to engine repairs. I say *repair* rather than *service* for French mechanics will have no problem in providing a service: but spare parts are spare parts and the English motor companies have still not managed to get a good distributive foothold in France. So if you have an English motor you should reckon to buy some spares to take care of the commoner ailments.

Deck Space

A major factor which should influence your choice is the provision of deck space, for in France you can expect to spend much more time outside than in. Many British cruisers have, in my opinion, far too little uncluttered deck space in which you can put a lilo or folding chairs and table. I remember once seeing an English party of six in a 32ft motor-sailer: they were all standing like sardines in the small cockpit —the rest of the deck was taken up with gear of every kind. This is not a success, especially in a hot climate.

Converting a Barge

If you like to live in spacious surroundings there is a great deal to be said for buying an old barge hull and—unless you have a stack of money—converting it yourself. But this is strictly for the handyman with plenty of time and a sufficiently prosperous piggy-bank to buy the large amount of raw materials you will need. There are a few such barges already converted around the waterways of France, Belgium and Holland and if you are lucky a 20-metre hull may not cost you any more than the price of a six-berth motor cruiser of a fraction the size. If you want to see hulls (price anywhere between £50 and £3,000) go to Rotterdam, Ghent and Antwerp. The choice is staggering. Large ones only (39 metre) at Conflans St Honorine on the Seine to the west of Paris. There are also possibilities with steel-hulled pontoons.

Inboard v Outboard

Engines always pose a dilemma. In theory there is much to be said for outboard motors. In the event of a breakdown you can lift them out and see what is up, in contrast to some inboard engines where attention can only be provided by a double-jointed man standing on his head. An outboard motor's propellers are easy to free from weed and they have no leaky stern-tubes. And you can take it home with you to service and winterise—if you are travelling by car. This allows you to be reasonably sure of a smart getaway when you return for your next cruise. But in reality they are not, in my view, as good as a *good* inboard. Outboard motors seem to be harder to start, make more noise, take substantially more fuel of an expensive grade, break down more often and are consequently more expensive to maintain. Yet because they are simpler to install (and therefore reduce the final cost) most of the smaller cruisers are constructed for propulsion by means of an outboard.

A compromise lies in the Z-drive system which claims to offer the advantages of both inboard and outboard, at impressively great expense. I am far from being convinced that it in fact does.

Most hire companies settle in the end for inboard motors, which perhaps speaks for itself. Certainly they are my recommendation.

Petrol v Diesel

If you possibly can afford the extra, you will always be pleased you installed a diesel engine. They are not only more reliable and *far* cheaper to run but also much safer, as they eliminate the possibility of explosive petrol fumes lying in the bilges.

Power

Since the speed regulations enforce a slow progress there is no point in looking for a sleek hull and powerful engine. Except in conditions of flood the only place you will be able to exploit the potential of such a boat is travelling upstream on the Rhône or in the short stretches of river reserved for speedboats or water-skiing.

Hull Form

Another factor worth a thought concerns the shape of the hull in relation to ice damage. Vertical sides are more likely to be crushed than rounded or V-form construction: these latter tend to be forced up *above* the ice.

One or Two Engines?

A boat with two screws is not suitable for the French waterways. In locks with sloping sides one screw may easily lodge on the rough masonry and come to grief. For this reason many good sea or coastal cruisers with two engines are not ideal for the inland waterways unless fitted with retractable screws or tip-up outboard motors.

Security

If you are planning to leave your boat unattended in France for weeks at a time, do study the matter of security. Some boats lock up neatly, making it quite difficult for the merely curious to effect an entry, though in France the chances of your suffering a break-in of this kind are fairly remote—provided you are outside the large cities.

Financing the Purchase

Just as with house purchase you can get bank advances or mortgages against the security of the boat.

Maintenance

Don't forget maintenance and caretaking. You may be able to do this yourself but if not, allow a little extra in your budget over and above the amount the boatyard tells you it will cost.

Insurance

Insurance also needs to be brought into the budget. Obtain several quotations. The annual premium for an average four-berth motor cruiser is about £20–£30.

How to Start

The best method of finding your way through the jungle of companies who make or sell boats and marine equipment in England, and those who provide services of one kind or another, is to buy copies of the better specialist magazines on the subject. There are several good ones (at any bookstall) and their purchase will be more than repaid by the knowledge they impart. You will be amazed by the manner in which your requirements are met. For truth to tell, you will not be the only person thinking of messing around in a boat!

Perhaps the biggest decision is not *which* boat to buy but *whether* to buy at all. Once over this hurdle everything else tends to drop into place.

PLANNING YOUR CRUISE

If a Frenchman asked your advice on where to cruise in England you might easily recommend the Thames or the Norfolk Broads—because they are established cruising grounds on the grand scale. No such equivalents exist in France. So, in helping you decide where to start, it is probably best to apply a gradual process of elimination. The crux of the matter is the area you prefer to see and, in making recommendations in this respect, I am on dangerous, highly subjective ground.

Of the waterways themselves—as distinct from their areas —it is almost useless to ask the advice of a Frenchman or the French Tourist Offices; apart from bargees, I have met only one Frenchman who had more than a superficial knowledge of the canal and river network.

None the less, if pressed to make some generalisations I would offer that, in my view, all the waterways which lie to the south of the navigable Seine (whether toward the west in Brittany or the east in Alsace) make excellent cruising areas. Above this east–west line I would add the canalised Meuse

(*Canal de l'Est*), the *Canal des Ardennes* and the upper reaches of the Marne. I would also hazard the observation that, in the end, you will not mind where you chose: it will almost certainly delight you—for each region has its own charms—and you can always move along to a new cruising ground for the next journey.

You must choose whether you want upland or lowland cruising, canal or river, pastoral or urban, hot or cool, busy or peaceful, long or short. You must decide whether you need epicurean food or just plain country cooking—or your own. And whether you want to tie up at night at the edge of a water-meadow with cows hock-deep in the clear water. Or moor at a smart quay to chance your hand at a casino and saunter back through the dawn to bed. It may help to refer to Appendix E ('Waterways Synopsis'), but there is really no substitute for poring over the appropriate Michelin maps from which you can gauge with some accuracy the general topography of the country through which you will be passing. From these you can also glean a mass of other information such as local places of interest, whether the waterway is too near a main road or a railway, whether it is wooded or open and so on. Bear in mind the remarks on weather in Chapter Four, and see Appendix H *Maps and Publications*.

When you have made a general choice of area, the advice which follows may help you to narrow your sights. If you are planning to make day cruises or to take a hotel boat you should consult Appendix C ('Cruise Operators'). Similarly, if you wish to hire a cruiser you should relate the possibilities to the advice in this chapter. But if you are using your own boat you need, of course, first to get to the cruising ground.

Sailing it across the Channel will obviously make serious inroads into a fortnight's holiday and you will not make much of any of the general areas I have recommended. So, if you have only this short time, I would suggest, in order of preference, the Ille–Rance–Villaine waterway of Brittany, the Seine and the *Canal de la Somme*. If you want a round trip

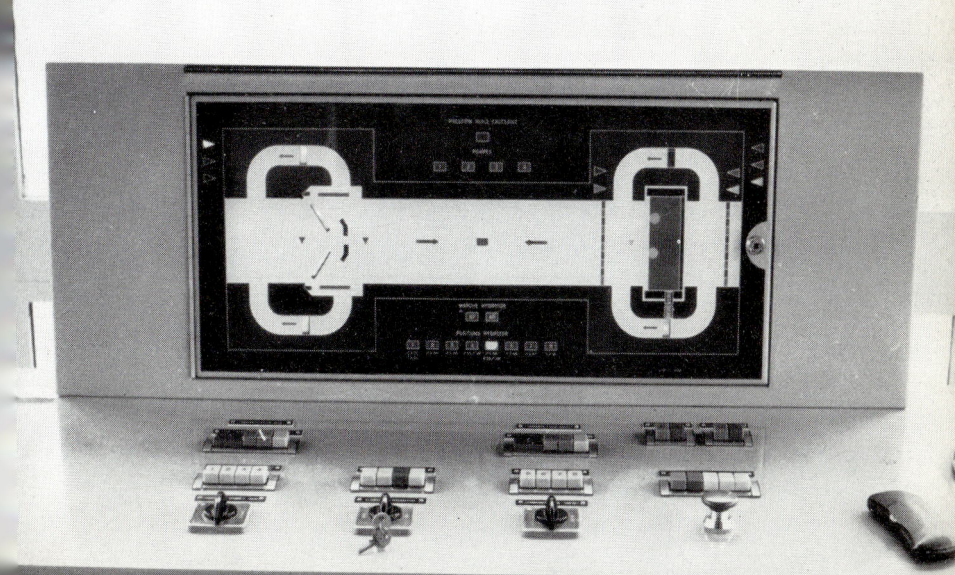

Page 35 (*above*) 2,000 ton capacity lock on the Seine; (*below*) the control panel for the lock

Page 36 (*above*) Looking down the 90 foot drop of the Bollène lock on the Rhône; (*below*) heavy shipping on the Seine, south of Paris

you might just accomplish in a fortnight the Somme, *Canal du Nord*, Oise and Seine or a two-way Seine journey to Paris. But such a busy itinerary would not be for me—nor, I suspect, after the first hectic day or so, for you either.

You really have the best possibilities—unless you have plenty of time—if you can tow your boat on a trailer to the selected area. You have greater flexibility this way—not only of cruising ground but also of cutting your journey to fit your diary. If you decide to linger you will not be committed to a round journey.

There is no map published showing the siting of launching-ramps for trailered boats so that for specific advice (of which French officialdom is very cautious) you will need to write to the regional office of the *Ponts et Chaussées* (see Appendix D: 'Inland Waterways Local Authorities'). But as a rule of thumb it is fairly safe to assume that any river town will be suitably equipped and that many canal towns will not be. So if you aim to start or finish on a canal and you cannot obtain specific assurances you may need to hunt around quite a bit for a suitable launching place. If you have taken your boat to the selected area by trailer you will of course have to return to your car at the end of your cruise. It is as well, therefore, to plan to start from near a railway station.

Another way of getting your boat to the chosen spot is by employing the services of a yacht 'deliverer'. There are 'professionals' at about £10 a day, plus fares and expenses (for a crew of two) and 'amateurs' who might make the trip for expenses only. Some of the larger British yacht builders maintain registers of interested crewmen. In my view the second alternative leaves far too much to chance and, unless your pockets are especially well lined, you may regret the expense of either course. Yet another way is to hire road transport. You will pay about 20p or 30p a return mile, plus the cost of taking the boat to and from the water.

Finally, there is the railway. Providing your boat 'section' does not exceed 8ft × 8ft you can hire a flat wagon. Approxi-

C   37

mate cost Le Havre to Marseilles would be £30 per ton for a two-ton boat; Marseilles to Lyon, about half that amount. Terminal operations would be extra. For longer boats you would need to contact the *Bureau des Transport Exceptionels*, or French Railways (see Appendix B: 'Useful Addresses'). If yours is a small boat—so small that it does not exceed a height of 5ft *on its trailer* it can be carried on the car sleeper trains at normal car tariff. This way it can cost as little as £10 for a Channel crossing.

In my experience people almost always go less far than they think they will. Not necessarily because of unforseen difficulties, but for the excellent reason that a growing lethargy overtakes them. Their daily progress declines. For me an ideal day's cruise is about three or four kilometres and takes in one lock. But I may be an extreme example! To work out the time it will take you to travel a canal or river, you should divide the total distance (see Appendix E) by the permitted speeds on the waterways concerned (see Appendix A for speed limits)—in order to work out the cruising hours you need to complete the distance. An average of half an hour (45 minutes in the north) has then to be added for each lock (again, see Appendix E). Even if you are the 'pressing-on' type of navigator, you would do well—even if, as you read this you think otherwise—to add 10 per cent to the total time you set aside for the journey in order to take care of contingencies. Then add, for each day, an hour for lunch and another for shopping or seeing the sights and so on.

Most people seem to find that four to six hours a day at the wheel is a pleasant average to maintain. I cannot advise you too strongly at this planning stage to limit ruthlessly your intended cruise distance. It is better by far to do a shorter length peacefully, amicably and thoroughly, than to see how far you can go. If you feel that it will be boring to make small progress, I suspect you will be amazed to find how completely the scenery changes with the slightest progress.

If you are taking children they will certainly want to linger:

exploring gravel pits, streams, villages and scrap-heaps is a children's paradise.

When you have selected your cruising area it is almost essential to buy the large-scale Michelin maps of the area. These are the series numbering from 51–86 or 2km to 1cm. You will need only one or two and the small cost is repaid many times by the interest and accuracy they provide. *Navigator's Guide* (see Appendix H) incorporates strip maps of each waterway—a great help in planning a cruise.

Some Hazards

There are on the French waterways—as on all canalised rivers and canals—stoppages (known as *chômages*). These are periods when a section of the waterway is closed for repair or maintenance. Each year, in about March, a list is published showing the affected places and the dates. Normally the summer months are the worst hit. It is foolish to formulate a plan without consulting this list. You risk being completely stuck or having to return. It can be obtained from the *Ministère de l'Equipement et du Logement* or *l'Office National de la Navigation*—see Appendix B for the address. If you are still facing a dilemma about which route to follow, this may help you eliminate some of the options.

Drought is a possible hazard. The worst months are September, October and November. The canals most often affected are the canals of Burgundy (Bourgogne), Centre, Nivernais, Marne au Rhin, de l'Est (branche Sud), Rhône au Rhin and the River Rhône. These waterways are only closed under conditions of exceptional drought. However, on these canals the depth is often reduced during this period or in the late summer, usually to about 1m60 (5ft 3in). On the Rhône the normal depth of 1m80 (5ft 11in) is often reduced to 1m10 (3ft 7in) during the period August to January. (See Appendix E.)

If you are thinking of descending the Rhône you should bear in mind the problem of getting back up the river again. Unlike any other navigable river in France, the Rhône is swift (up to 10 knots) and you may need a tow from one of the powerful Rhône barges. This is likely to cost £100 and the arrangements are not easily made.

Floods are sometimes encountered from November to March. These can affect river navigation though they are seldom so bad that traffic is halted altogether. But without experience and a good engine these conditions are not recommended. The canals are spared the floods but in turn suffer from ice. Apart from the waterways of the far South, ice is a normal occurrence in January or February and navigation is often suspended during cold spells of a week or so.

On the French waterways, unlike the British, width is most unlikely to be a problem, though if you are the owner of a Thames sailing barge or a steam yacht you should study carefully the critical dimensions listed in Appendix E.

If you are not prepared to navigate in the rain, I make no comment other than to recommend that you allow a good margin of extra time. Even in the south it *can* rain.

Although weed is unusual on the French waterways, in the polluted rivers like the Seine you should allow time occasionally for removing polythene bags and less pleasant things from your propeller!

One major consideration is the view from the waterway. Most French rivers have a very variable flow, particularly in the southern half. This means that in summer, when the water tends to be low, you may not get a good view across the adjacent countryside. In the northern half of France the upper Marne also suffers from this disadvantage. But if the cockpit floor or the crews' 'sun-deck' is four or five feet above water level it will usually be high enough.

EQUIPMENT

This will depend on your mode of travel. If you have chosen a canoe all you will need is a miniature camping outfit. And if you are hiring a cruiser you will see from the hirers' inventory that little or nothing need be brought. So I address myself to the adventurer who intends to use his own craft. Much will depend on the space at your disposal but all the following pieces of equipment will, I think, be worth close consideration.

If you are bringing your craft across by sea you will need a good deal of additional equipment: charts, dividers, parallel ruler, flares, radar reflector, RDF compass and log—but I assume that if you are coming this way you will either be used to sea-cruising procedure or have someone with you who is.

Life-Jackets

First things first. Lifebelts or life-jackets? Providing you can swim well it is not usual to wear life-jackets on the inland waterways. But for non-swimmers, and especially for children, life-jackets are basic sense. For adults and older children the best solution is the type of life-jacket that can be inflated by a toggle-operated gas cylinder. These are the least cumbersome. For small children I think there is no substitute for something which is permanently inflated or inherently buoyant. Small children unable to swim, even though life-jacket equipped, are best tethered by a harness and dog-lead to a fixed steel line stretched fore and aft along the deck—if you have room for such an arrangement. Otherwise if they are running loose you will constantly be worried that they may have dropped over the edge, and in a lock this is a very bad worry indeed. For such children you should insist that they wear their life-jackets even when you have stopped and even, yes even, when they are playing on the bank.

Dinghy

The next most obvious piece of life-saving equipment is a dinghy. You may think that on a waterway there is something humorous about a lifeboat and on a canal this may be so, but you may equally well be on a broad river. If you are unfortunate enough to have a collision midstream you could be very glad of a lifeboat. This is particularly true in the tidal reaches of rivers

41

where the banks can be of mud so soft that you sink to your waist or higher when you try to climb out. A dinghy which is to double as a lifeboat is, of course, only of value if it can be launched immediately. Often one sees dinghies so well secured that there would be little or no chance of releasing them in an emergency. They must be instantly detachable.

Although I have presented the dinghy as a piece of life-saving equipment its main role will, I sincerely hope, be for shopping or crossing to the other side of a river—it is surprisingly useful not to have to unmoor and remoor a larger boat, and great fun to explore tributaries. Children amuse themselves for long periods in a dinghy—particularly when they can also bathe. Of course a smaller cruiser has precious little room to accommodate one and it is best dispensed with altogether. Inflatable dinghies are, however, a possible solution here. Don't forget the oars!

Some people seem to derive satisfaction from a dinghy with a small outboard motor. I do not share their feelings. One motor (to go wrong) is quite sufficient. The trouble and noise deter me and when mine was finally stolen I was delighted!

A last word on dinghies: do not tow them. It may seem the obvious solution to the storage problem and you will sometimes see it demonstrated. Everything goes well until an emergency stop unites the tow line with the propeller. If the line does not break, nor the propeller stop, the dinghy will be wound into the propeller, with predictable results. I came across just such an instance in Rouen. When the dinghy—of solid construction—met the propeller, the blades stopped rotating instantly. Instead the engine left its mountings and tore a hole in the side of the boat. It only took a few minutes to sink . . . The idea of towing a dinghy alongside, as a means of avoiding this last eventuality, is only to move from the frying-pan into the fire, for it will soon be crushed.

Cordage

Whatever name you use to describe the article known to laymen as rope, you should ensure you have enough of it. Visit a ship's chandler and see the many varieties available and you will find tables to help you calculate the grade you require for the weight of your boat. Some ropes sink in water, others float. Some stretch, others hardly expand at all. There are many technical considerations and it is wise to reflect on these with the product (and price list) in front of you. Terylene has provided my best investment.

Do not economise on length. For a 2 ton 25ft cruiser, I would recommend at least 2 60ft lengths and 1 of 90ft; for a 7-ton boat at least 4 90ft lengths. As a refinement you can have shock-resistant ropes for use in locks (these stretch) and stretch-resistant ones for mooring. Some of the cheaper plastic ropes stretch like elastic and in places where you need a secure mooring they can be a thorough nuisance.

Boathook

Next, make sure you have a good boathook—as long a one as you can conveniently stow. You may even be glad of two— particularly if you have run aground.

Siren

A loud siren, horn or hooter is essential, besides being obligatory. The most practical solution is the aerosol compressed-air type with renewable containers. They produce an eminently satisfactory noise.

Fenders

Fenders in many elegant shapes and sizes can be found at a chandler's, but you cannot beat a motor tyre. For the smaller boat an old Mini tyre is ideal. It costs nothing, hardly shows the dirt and takes much more punishment than any elegant sausage or coir fender. The best way to hang tyres is to make

2 ¾in holes about 4in apart in the centre of the tread. Through these you can thread the rope with which you secure the tyre. If you put it round the tyre, the rope will chafe against the lock walls. For a 27ft cruiser you can usefully do with 4 tyres a side. And it is a good idea, if you have the space, to keep one extra on a 6ft length of line, so that you can quickly insert it at an unprotected spot when the need arises.

Motor-tyre fenders virtually double as bathing ladders, providing a conveniently placed step for clambering out of the water.

Flags

Always a touchy subject, but suffice it to say that flag etiquette is fairly loose on the waterways. No flag-hauling ceremony is to be observed amongst the bargees at sunset. However, everyone wears his national flag at the stern (the red ensign for most of us) and it is definitely polite to fly the *tricolor* from the bow. A flag at the bow is also useful as a wind indicator.

Drinking Water

You may have to last a few days without being able to replenish your water tanks—at least not without carrying cans a longish way—so adequate water storage is important.

Drinking water in towns is usually good but in some of the country districts it can be a little suspect. The French seldom drink it, preferring—as do many English—*vin du pays* or in an emergency the many varieties of bottled water which are available everywhere.

Fuel

Extra containers for fuel are also useful, though all grades are well distributed. If you have a paraffin-burning refrigerator you will need a special kind of highly-refined paraffin of which the best known variety is called Kerdane. Since this is usually unobtainable in small towns it is worth storing a reasonable quantity. Be very careful: the French for paraffin is *pétrôle*. The confusion has cost lives.

Miscellaneous

A searchlight is useful, not just for tunnels but for illuminating one's way to the café or for checking the moorings at night.

A plank (or even a ladder) is useful, both as a gangway and for hanging outside the tyres when moored alongside piles. A hose for filling your water tanks is a luxury: it takes up so much space and often there is one provided. If you do have room for one you may well be glad of it on occasion but it needs to be at least 100ft in length. A universal rubber fitting for the end is essential.

Other equipment which can justify taking up valuable space includes funnels, a torch, candles, an assortment of tools (in accordance with your skill and the likelihood of extensive repairs), spares for the engine, pickets and sledge hammer, rags, a bucket or two, a rubbish bucket with lid, field glasses and useful everyday things like string shopping-bags, scissors, self-adhesive tape, string, and so on. If you have room, but not at the expense of vast inconvenience, there is a strong case for a bicycle. Distances are great in France and even a short walk with two baskets of bottles and provisions is not much fun. And on a Monday the baker who is open tends to be the one in the next village!

A fire extinguisher, besides being obligatory, is a sensible addition. And the same applies to a first-aid box.

Gas Cylinders

Butane gas cylinders are plentifully distributed throughout France. If your cooker, heater or refrigerator is gas-operated, you should be very careful. You will doubtless already know that this gas is heavier than air, that it can hang around in the bilges and, on being offered a spark or a flame, may explode. French gas fittings are sometimes different—so you need to be very careful indeed. Inspect the joints frequently and always

45

turn off the supply *at the cylinder* (which should be stowed on deck). When you turn in at night, never leave a gas fire burning.

Undoubtedly the best answer to the cooking and heating problem is to obtain equipment which burns diesel oil. This is standard practice in France amongst the larger craft, and if you have a diesel engine it provides you not only with the safest solution but the most convenient as well. For one tank supplies all requirements.

Rubbish Disposal

Rubbish disposal is a problem. Except along the busier quays where provision for rubbish collection is sometimes made, the stuff is usually tipped into the water. Indeed, the only alternative is to litter the bank with it. Clearly there is a problem here and a moral duty as well. The unforgivable sin must be to throw into the water anything which will pollute it. I do not mean empty tins or chop bones. I mean substances like oil or detergent. These are the things which alter the chemistry of nature. They kill the fish, the birds that eat them and the plant life. When the contaminated effluent reaches the sea the process continues—the plankton die, then the fish and thus... to total extinction. Whole seas, like the Mediterranean, are already threatened with irreversible pollution. And do not think that one small oil slick will not make any difference to the balance of nature; one extra straw broke the camel's back! In this permissive age it is considered almost Victorian to use the word *wicked*. But this adjective is entirely appropriate for those who defy this rule.

Let us be clear. Pollution of canals and rivers has nothing to do with litter. Plastic bottles floating on the surface may be unsightly and to put them there may be thoughtless, selfish and uncivilised. But it threatens nothing.

A solution to the problem is this: Perishable commodities like food-remains are unceremoniously tipped overboard to the advantage of mariner and fish alike. Objects which will sink: tin cans, bottles (first filled with water), join the perish-

46

ables—not an ideal solution but not too bad either: the cans soon rust away and the bottles break up in the rivers and, ultimately, become shiny translucent pebbles and, in the canals, are eventually dredged out; though glass bottles are clearly not for tipping in places likely to be used by bathers and should always be sunk unbroken in deep water. The semi-perishables, like cereal packets, wrappers and so on are saved up and at intervals burnt at a convenient place on the bank.

Fire is also used to dispose of sump oil and greasy rags. This just leaves plastic containers and these are a hideous nuisance. If you cannot avoid buying them again, it is best to save them and, if you cannot find a litter bin (or a rubbish dump) poke them down rabbit holes: an inconvenience for the rabbits but it is their contribution to solving the human rather than the rabbit litter problem! Try not to buy bottled water in plastic bottles. There are still some brands using glass ones.

Never throw rope into the water. It is not a pollutant and may not even float but it can easily wrap itself around the propellers of barges. Similarly, if you lose a rubber-tyre fender you should retrieve it—it can jam in the propeller tunnels of barges and is a nightmare to remove.

Last, but not least, the lavatory. The system known as direct discharge, though not ideal, is normal on the Continent. Chemical closets are not widely used. From a functional stand-point the type which is 'gravity operated' is preferable to the sort which is operated by a pump—though this is a necessary evil if the equipment is below water level.

IMPORT FORMALITIES

Temporary Importation of Boats
1. Pleasure craft without motors and not exceeding 5·5 metres (18ft) in length may be temporarily imported, without formality, as personal effects.
2. Pleasure craft without motors and more than 5·5 metres (18ft) in length, sailing boats, and craft with motors may

47

be temporarily imported by *ferry* under cover of a *carnet de passage* or a *triptyque*, both of which permits are valid for a period of six months. To obtain this documentation you should apply to the Automobile Association or the Touring Club of France. (See Appendix B for addresses.)

3. When the vessels listed under 2 above are imported by *sea*, a passport for foreign pleasure boats, or an *acquit à caution*, is issued by the Customs at the first port of call. The passport is valid for one year from the date of issue, but the total length of time spent in France under the temporary importation regulation may not be more than six months a year. No deposit is required.

On arrival by sea from abroad and before leaving for another country, the owner or user of a pleasure craft must declare his arrival or departure at the port Customs office. Declaration to the Customs on arrival must be indicated: during the day, by hoisting the 'DIF' signal or, failing this, the yellow Q flag of the international code of signals; at night, either by illuminating the signal used during the day, or by showing a red light over a white light (these lights must not be more than 1.83 metres (6ft) apart). These signals must remain visible until Customs formalities have been completed. The Customs will visa the passport issued for the craft. The passport may be used for several successive journeys abroad while it remains valid.

4. The passport, or *carnet de passage*, is issued only to foreign pleasure craft belonging to people normally residing outside France, and on condition that these craft be used only privately for the personal needs of those who are allowed to benefit from the temporary import regulations. They may not be used for profit-making, or lent, hired or sold to anyone principally resident in France. The *carnet de passage* can normally be 'suspended' by surrendering it to the Customs at the end of a journey. In this way the six months limit can be stretched substantially, if you plan a series of short cruises.

(This regulation is not at present generally appreciated and at the time of writing this book I found no travel or tourist organisation familiar with the meaning of this rule. The French Tourist Office has given permission for this letter to be quoted:

> I have pleasure to inform you that your boat can be left in France for any period of time without incurring import duty nor TVA, provided the owner or user of the said boat does not remain in France for more than six months in any one year and provided he leaves the boat passport with the local Customs Office before leaving France.
>
> Port, in the legal sense, should be understood as a place where a boat can be left and where the Customs have an official representation.

See also this chapter: 'Where and How to Leave your Boat'.)
5. There are no special taxes to be paid.

Permanent Importation of Boats

In cases of permanent importation, Customs duty must be paid, but no licence is required.

Further particulars on customs formalities can, if required, be obtained from the *Bureau des Douanes pour le Tourisme* (see Appendix B).

PERMITS

Permis de Navigation

This is required only for boats fitted with an engine of more than 10hp BUT foreigners (eg Britons) are required to comply only with the existing laws of their own country and, providing this is done, the *permis de navigation* requirement is waived.

Permis de Conduire or driving licence

The same comments apply as for the *permis de navigation*.

Permits for driving boats hired in France

Provided the boat is hired from a boat-hire company (and not, for example, from a private individual) you need only give an undertaking that your proficiency in the type of craft hired satisfies your own country's laws. If you are unable to do this you should write to the intending hire company for advice.

Permis de Circulation or Circulation Permit

This is required for the navigation of all canals and most canalised rivers. Moreover it is a document that will be repeatedly asked for by lock-keepers (who enter their stamp in the spaces provided) and it should therefore be preserved carefully. There are, however, certain exceptions for which this document is not required. These are:

(a) All rivers without locks,

(b) Seine, Marne, Oise, Aisne.

To obtain this document you should apply to the *Ministère de l'Equipement* (see Appendix B for address). You will be sent a form to fill. Since this is in French, the following is a translation of the questions in the order in which they are listed.

> Name of boat owner
> Nationality
> Address
> Address to which permit should be sent
> Name of boat
> *Itinerary
> Place of your arrival in France
> Dates of journey
> Length of boat overall (but with rudder sideways, if applicable)
> Beam overall
> Draught laden
> Air draught unladen (mast stepped, if applicable)
> Signature.

*The Itinerary should list the rivers or canals to be navigated.

The form may be completed in English. The *Permis de Circulation* will exempt you from paying any lock dues except on the Moselle downstream of Thionville.

Certificat de Capacité

This is a document no longer normally required by skippers of small boats. It corresponds to a pilot's licence and you should, in any case, have a pilot on board on the occasions when it is needed.

As you will now see, the actual 'formalities' for a foreigner cruising in France are, to say the least, minimal.

You may find that the information given above is at variance with the instruction given in older publications or current tourist information sheets. I have yet to see all the facts stated correctly in any publication of British origin. Since you could be greatly inconvenienced by wrong documentation and since 'formalities' are subject to revision, you will be safest if you contact the *Ministère de l'Equipement et du Logement* (see Appendix B) and ask for the latest edition of *'Navigation de Plaisance sur les Eaux Intérieures'*. It is issued free.

WHERE AND HOW TO LEAVE YOUR BOAT

Assuming that you intend to surrender your six-months entry permit, you will need to find a suitable place to leave your boat. If you have decided that you wish to use your boat in France for periods exceeding six months per annum, then you must apply to the authorities for payment of duty and TVA.

To anyone used to the crowded conditions of the English waterways, the problem of a protracted mooring may loom as a potential worry. But in fact it is fairly simple. When mooring for a day or so it is necessary merely to find a place where you are not going to impede the traffic—and tie up! It is, however, a good idea to tell the adjacent lock-keeper when you will be back, just in case the canal or river engineer-in-charge wonders if the boat is permanently moored.

For longer stays of, say, a week or two, unless there is someone left aboard, you should seek permission from the engineer responsible for the particular waterway. The lock-keeper will tell you where he can be contacted and may offer to contact him for you. It is unwise to moor for long periods in rivers if the boat is unattended. The water level can vary quickly and substantially.

To moor for the winter or for a prolonged period you will need the permission of the regional Director of the *Ponts et Chaussées* (see Appendix D for addresses). If you know where you plan to stop, it is wise to seek permission in advance as it can save you time at the end of your journey. In any event, do not leave the arrangements until the last day as it is possible that if repairs are planned for the waterway you are on it may be necessary for you to move on a substantial distance. The *Ponts et Chaussées* authorities will direct you to the nearest place out of the way of traffic and where canal repairs and maintenance are not envisaged during the period of your absence. They will want you to leave the boat in such a way that it will not give any trouble; that is to say, it must be properly moored and there should be someone 'responsible' to answer for it in the event of its having to be moved.

This sounds more frightening than it is likely to be. It is, after all, a reasonable requirement on the part of the authorities. Actually, it has never taken me long to find someone willing to 'take the keys' though you may wish to give some financial inducement to this person—in my experience, however, this has seldom been actually requested.

Obviously the degree of responsibility you are able to establish will depend on the person you have found and the sort of boat you have. If you are trying to leave a sea-going ship, possession of the keys may be about all you are able to arrange. But if it is a two-ton motor cruiser you will probably have not the least difficulty in arranging for regular inspection,

Page 53 (*above*) Aqueduct carrying feeder stream to the Nivernais Canal at Montreuillon; (*below*) a lock house—and a prettier use for motor car tyres

Page 54 (*above*) One of the last horse-drawn barges on the Canal Latéral à la Loire; (*below*) one of the last electric traction 'horses', now defunct

bilge emptying, ice breaking and even hand-towing to the other side of the lock in the case of emergency.

The great thing to bear in mind in making such arrangements is that you will probably be asking for something never previously requested. Consequently it can be fatal to 'rush' your selected caretaker into assuming responsibility for what to him may, momentarily, seem a frightening assignment. A slow chat over a glass of wine will be more effective than the promise of great monetary reward.

So far as inducement or reward is concerned, something like £1 a week is the kind of figure for the services I have mentioned—plus a 'float' of £10 to cover an emergency like the repair of a broken window. It is a good plan, for your peace of mind, to leave your caretaker with a small supply of stamped, addressed envelopes so that he can write to you at intervals to confirm that both he and your boat are still in existence. But remember, there is absolutely no obligation on the part of the lock-keeper (or whomever you have been referred to) to accept this responsibility so, initially at least, you are asking a favour.

In making these arrangements it is most certainly a great help to have some knowledge of the language but many people manage perfectly well without it.

It is up to you to inform the local Customs office of your actions so that your boat 'passport' or *Carnet* may be surrendered. The Customs may wish to 'seal' your boat—a ritual which involves the Customs Officer travelling (at your expense) from the nearest Customs Office to the mooring and tying a piece of thin string from the wheel to some other fixed point, the knot having a lead seal crimped over it. It is normal for the wash of the first boat passing to cause sufficient movement to the steering gear for the string to be broken!

It will be difficult and I think undesirable to leave your boat for the winter without incurring some expense. So if you have to budget £30 to £50 for this each year, remember that you are probably saving an equivalent amount by not having your boat on an English waterway. For here you would be paying an annual waterway licence and mooring charges which together can very readily equal this kind of sum.

If you have a boat which can easily be taken from the water, this is the obvious thing to do. You can then leave it with a garage or even, by arrangement, with a lock-keeper and there is no risk of it having to be moved. For it should be made clear that canals do, occasionally, have to be emptied at short notice, and if you are unable to make satisfactory arrangements for the removal of your boat by a local person, the ultimate responsibility will be with you to go and move it yourself. In any event, you will still need to arrange for 'immobilisation' by the Customs.

CHAPTER THREE

Afloat

THE OPEN ROAD—CANALS

In writing these notes I must assume, in order to avoid duplication, that you are familiar with the Rules of the Road, the common signals and the other main points covered in this book. In your own interest therefore, if this is not the case, you should absorb this information before you start since you may need some of it within a short time of leaving the quay. Let us start with canals; they are easier than rivers.

The main hazard—if this is not too strong a word—including locks, bridges, quays and moorings (which are dealt with separately) is meeting other traffic. There are two points to bear in mind.

You may suddenly see the massive black bows of an unladen barge appear, at speed, around a blind corner. I say *see* rather than *hear* because you are unlikely to notice the oncoming barge's engine above the noise of your own. Even if you are in a rowing boat it may still come as a surprise: noise plays peculiar tricks on water. Your immediate reaction may be to doubt that there could possibly be room for both of you. Since the barge is unlikely to slow down you may feel drawn toward performing some demonstrative action like waving your arms and shouting.

Don't. You will be wasting effort and the bargee is most unlikely to be deflected from his purpose. If he continues

57

toward you it is because there *is* room. But he will assume that you know how to pass him. (Just occasionally, there are narrow passages, usually very short, and in a few of these there is a distinct shortage of width. If you cannot see to the far end it may be sensible to walk ahead and investigate.) The worst thing you can do is to switch off and wallow directionless in the middle of the canal. This could promote a crisis since barges can need several hundred yards in which to stop.

As the oncoming boat moves toward you, you should keep about a third of the way across the canal from the right-hand bank, with just enough speed to give good steerage. An unladen barge will also probably be keeping to starboard but, if laden, it may very well be dead centre. Do not jump to the conclusion that the skipper is of fatherless origin: a heavily laden barge needs depth often found only in the very centre of a cut.

When you are separated by a hundred or so yards move over rather more to the right-hand side so as to give plenty of margin. At the same time apply a little more speed to give you increased manoeuvrability because as you come up to the oncoming barge you will find a tendency—especially if it is laden—first to be pushed toward the bank and then, as you pass, to be drawn towards it. To counteract these tendencies you need some power—and increased manoeuvrability. It is a mistake to hug the side too closely. You risk damaging your boat on projecting obstacles or even fouling your propeller—and then becoming helpless.

Overtaking a moving barge should not be attempted within a mile of a lock, unless you are invited by hand signals to do so, and it is your responsibility to see there is sufficient room for the operation without running the risk of blocking the canal to oncoming traffic.

You will soon become happy about meeting other traffic. The first encounter is by far the worst. (See also 'Rules for Passing and Overtaking' in Chapter Five.)

As you approach corners—and some *are* remarkably blind

58

—you should obviously move with caution. Always expect a barge to appear at the most awkward moment: your expectation will occasionally be rewarded. And so much the better: it adds to the fun! Perhaps the blindest of all corners are those on which narrow bridges are placed. Extra caution is needed and if you have a long boat it can even be worth posting a look-out at the bow. The Midi Canal specialises in corners crossed by narrow humpback bridges.

Along the canals you will frequently encounter 'ports' or harbours. These are normally enlarged sections of canal which often have a quay for loading barges. You will also come across circular areas which are intended for turning barges. Many ports and turning areas have been abandoned by commercial navigation and are no longer maintained. So, before you are tempted into an attractive-looking basin, watch out for the tell-tale water-lily or rush breaking the surface. You may well find only a few inches of water covering six feet of soft mud. Taken at speed you may—as I sometimes have— pass an interesting hour or so extricating yourself.

The only other predictable canal hazard is the very rarely encountered point at which a canal traverses a river. This normally involves a short journey fairly near the lip of a weir and the remarks I have made under this heading in the following chapter should be heeded. With only a small current on the river (and as long as the engine keeps going!) there is little problem. As a rule, if the current is strong, as in times of flood, the crossing is closed—in any event there is normally a safety cable to prevent the worst occurring. At the most difficult of these crossings, that of the Loire at Decize, a towing service operates.

THE OPEN ROAD—RIVERS

The general rule in canalised rivers—in the absence of special notices or regulations—is to keep a distance of some 20yd from the towpath side.

But the bigger rivers are normally free of obstructions in the centre third of their width: such rivers are usually the subject of special charts in strip form (see Appendix H: 'Maps and Publications', for a list of such maps). In my experience, the possession of such charts makes for a peaceful mind though, to be sure, there are few enough real danger points on most rivers. Still, you only need to avoid going round the wrong side of an island and running aground or striking the top of a training wall, to make the purchase a sound investment.

For readers who are unfamiliar with the purpose of locks and weirs it may not be until you have read the chapter 'Why Locks?' that you will appreciate the part they play. To see the water cascading over a weir in a sizeable river and to hear its thunderous roar is surely to be impressed. The undesirability of passing this way in a boat becomes wonderfully apparent.

None the less, each year this is how a few people terminate their cruise. Why? Having very nearly been over one myself I shrink from giving 'stupidity' as the answer and compromise on the kindlier word: 'carelessness'. With reasonable attention to your map, and a tolerably sober and vigilant helmsman, you should never miss the lock-cut through which you should have passed. Even if you do, in all innocence, cruise steadily forward toward the weir, you only need to worry if you are going downstream. For in the other direction you will normally see the wall of water and, realising your error, turn about and pretend you were exploring. As you approach the weir— which may be anywhere from fifty yards to many miles from the missed lock-cut—you should still be in no real danger. Almost certainly there will be further warning signs. You *may* hear it, but do not rely on this, for weirs are notoriously difficult to hear when approached from upstream: the sound is thrown away from their faces.

You may be thinking that you are bound to see it. Indeed you probably will—or rather you may see the rows of needles (the cricket-bat shaped objects used for regulating the level) and almost certainly you will see the platform the weir keeper uses for walking across the river to insert or remove the needles. On the bigger weirs the flow of water is controlled by huge, mechanically operated shutters secured between massive towers high above the river. And very often a steel cable stretched across the river will prevent your being drawn over.

Still, it is only fair to say that there are weirs without the warning signs, the safety cables or any obvious accompanying structures. And in a light morning mist it is just possible that you will notice your error too late . . . yet even now you will probably be all right. If your boat has a reasonable draught or a keel and there is not too much water flowing, you are likely to come to rest against the sill. But if your luck is out and your boat is swept over the edge, you may have time to do little more than reach for a lifebelt; you will certainly need it!

In river cruising, if you have no chart and there is no tow-path, you should as a rule keep to the outside of the bends—that is to say, you should take the long way round the corner—for here the current will probably have dug the deepest channel. The rules for passing or overtaking remain the same, irrespective of your position in the river.

When using an anchor, remember to put out a length of rope or chain about three times the depth of the river. If you lower the anchor slowly you will easily feel when it touches the bottom. Before anchoring you should, if travelling downstream, turn to face upstream and come to rest moving gently down with the speed of the current. Anchoring is a convenient way of stopping for a bathe or for a meal but it is not a sound idea to anchor for the night. You can never be certain how firmly you are secured and you are unlikely to sleep soundly if you suspect that you may be drifting quietly toward a weir.

Never anchor in the navigable channel and remember that the wind can blow you round the anchor. If you have stopped with 20ft of water beneath you, you will (with three times this length of chain) be able to pivot nearly 60ft *either side* of the anchor. So you can see that you need a wide area in which to perform this manoeuvre. A good place is sometimes just beyond the entrance to a lock-cut—provided the weir is some way off!

A final point about rivers concerns the existence of 'training walls' or submerged dykes. Their purpose is to 'train' the current toward the centre of the river. They are usually encountered on the larger rivers, for which I have already suggested you buy a chart showing their existence clearly. Such walls are extremely solid and it will not be worth trying conclusions with them. You can sometimes see the point at which they enter the river and you can often detect a change in the flow of water on the surface above them, or even see a line of rushes growing from their crowns. But guessing at these walls is a poor game, however obvious *most* of them may be.

QUAYS, BRIDGES AND TUNNELS

Quays

There are two kinds: public and private, and it is as well to identify the one for which you are heading. Apart from being found in all towns of any size, many villages provide public quays and they are there for you to use. No one can tell you to move on so—unless a bargee needs the place for loading—once moored, you can relax. In many towns the public quays enjoy pride of place and you could not find a more convenient position for revictualling or seeing the sights. Often, in the evenings, the social life of the place develops here: the unmarried girls walk the length of the quay, in twos and threes, hoping to be seen by the teams of young *boules* players for whom the level ground offers ideal conditions. In the shade of spreading plane trees you can take your ease and watch life unfold around you.

Some quays have bollards. But more often they have rings, usually on top of the quay wall but sometimes set in the vertical face. In the villages, grass obscures these quay-top rings so that it is necessary to tramp about a bit to locate them.

It may be tempting to moor in front of steps, but remember

that these will be needed by others. Politeness also demands that you avoid making straight for a quay lined with the rods of attendant fishermen.

Two warnings. If you see a quay with a bite out of the edge, the missing piece is probably lying just below waiting to hole your hull! And, it may be worth mooring upstream of the town sewer.

Private quays are another matter. If they appear to be in regular use it is better not to push your luck: a bargee will hardly thank you if, at the end of a long day, he arrives to find you in his place. But you will see many quays which are abandoned and quite all right for you to use—unless there are warning notices.

Bridges

The fixed bridges present little or no difficulty so long as you are not nudging the height limit of the canal (see Appendix E). But if you are, there *may* be problems. The indicated height should not be taken as completely accurate; I have known errors of up to a foot.

New bridges over unfrequented canals are often culprits because their engineers have simply not bothered to respect the regulation clearance. But there are other variables: the abutments may have sunk, the water level may be unduly high (due to excess water being admitted, or oncoming traffic), or the span may even have sagged. Another potential problem for larger craft is that the advertised height refers sometimes to the apex of the arch (as opposed to the 'navigational rectangle') so that small, arched bridges can present difficulties for the outer edges of your superstructure.

It is as well to know that, if you are stuck by a few centimetres, you can normally gain sufficient clearance by asking the lock-keeper to let out some water from your pound. If it is a particularly low bridge he will be quite used to the request, though in times of water shortage he may not be able to oblige. So, if you are pushing the limits, you will be sensible to proceed with caution rather than rely on any figures you have been given—even in this book!

Moving bridges are quite frequent in France (though not as numerous as in Holland). There are two types, the first of which is a swing-bridge. As the name implies, the bridge swings round (at a right-angle to the canal) and, pivoted near one end of the span, leaves a gap for the navigation. Occasionally these swing from a central pivot so that you may be able to pass either side of the swung span. The other type is a lift-bridge, also known as a bascule. This is a bit like the medieval castle drawbridge and has been immortalised by Van Gogh's painting of the canal drawbridge near Arles.

Both kinds are operated by attendants unless worked by the adjacent lock-keeper, in which case you will see him mount a bicycle and ride along the towpath ahead of you as you leave the lock. To request operation of moving bridges, give one long blast on the hooter when you are near enough to be heard.

Tunnels

There are tunnels on many of the French waterways and each has its own character. Some have dimensions larger (and others smaller) than those of the canal they serve. Some have towpaths; others do not. Some are lined with smooth masonry; others present jagged rock. Some can only be passed as part of a towed convoy; others may be negotiated unaided. The specifications and characteristics are listed in Appendix F: 'Tunnels'.

Unless you are being hauled through the tunnel in a convoy (probably by an electrically-operated tug which pulls itself along on a heavy chain lifted from the bed of the canal, passed over the tug and dropped off again astern), you may have to make your own way in the company of barges whose progress can be pitifully slow owing to the effect of suction in narrow confines. In this case it is worth seeing whether you can go first or last, the former being preferable and normally acceptable since you will not hold up the barges if you can make three to four knots. If you are in a line of barges the fumes of their exhausts can be almost asphyxiating and the near total obscurity induced by these fumes makes it almost impossible to see anything, with the obvious risk of resultant damage.

A good light and a keen eye are essential to spot logs and driftwood floating on the surface of the water in tunnels. This is because some bargees make a practice of lashing sections of log between the forward bollards on one side and the stern bollards on the other, so that the projecting logs act as fenders. By placing the rudder to one side of centre, the barge will then take a central but oblique course, providing the logs do not break—which they often do! Unless you have very strong bollards the practice is not recommended.

Another vicissitude encountered in tunnels where tugs operate is the live electric wires from which they draw their power. In some of these tunnels the vault and the wires are sufficiently high not to cause a danger but in others special care must be taken.

It is sometimes cold in the tunnels and the vault often drips. A waterproof can be useful. Some people recommend the wearing of dark glasses before you enter a tunnel so that, when you take them off as you go in, the sudden contrast from light to dark is minimised and your vision improved.

But, in spite of its problems, its temperature and drips, a tunnel is fascinating—if a little eerie. No cruise is quite complete without one.

MOORING AND LANDING

It looks quite simple. It *is* simple. But the moorings which 'go wrong' are the cause of pain and grief to many a ship's captain—whose fault it usually is.

Mooring may be construed as the act of bringing a boat alongside land and tying a firm line from ship to shore. The finer points of the operation demand that:

—neither the hull nor the propellers should be damaged by sudden contact with solid objects;

—the place selected for the operation should provide at least a sporting chance for the crew to reach *terra firma* without having to swim for it;

—there should be something suitable to which to tie the boat;

—once tied, the knots will not slip;

—the securing arrangements should be such that the craft is not battered to death by the wash from passing boats.

You will agree that these demands seem reasonable enough. Yet experience shows that success in handling boats often stops short of a neat execution of these basic manoeuvres. So first, let us look at the principles of 'coming alongside'.

The approach of ship toward shore should, as a rule, be at a good angle, thus:

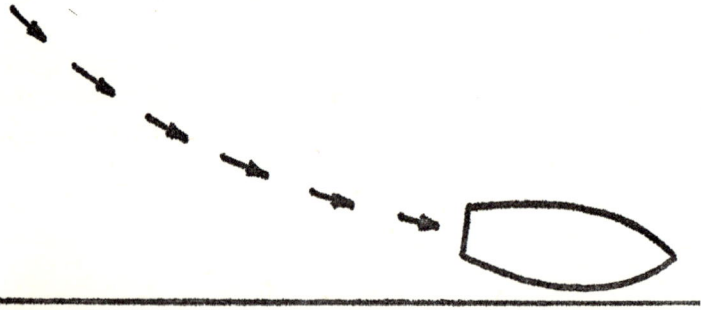

rather than:

This minimises the danger of fouling the boat on underwater obstacles near the edge. Similarly, it leaves the propeller in deeper water and enables it to be used until the end of the operation. When mooring in a river, the approach should always be upstream (against the current), otherwise you are likely to be carried beyond your intended landing place.

The last part of this manoeuvre needs to be examined in detail. When the boat is in something like the attitude of approach to the bank as drawn below,

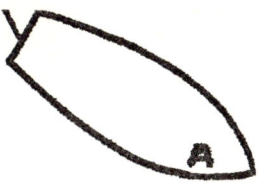

the member of the crew selected for mooring duty (usually the most agile from the ship's company!) is standing at the point marked A. At this moment there should be little or no way on the boat and the captain's skill lies in his ability to bring the bows to the selected place without either ramming the bank or stopping so short that the crew needs wings to cross the gap. A boathook can be of assistance here.

As soon as the bank is reached the crewman 'steps' ashore and makes fast, a detail to which I shall return. The point to observe here is that the mooring line should be attached either to the midships cleat (on a light boat only) or to the bow cleat. Under no circumstances should the rope be attached to the stern of the boat for if you are mooring in a river, facing upstream, the current is likely to swing the bow away from the bank and you will soon be in a mess. With the bow secured it is easy to bring in the stern either with the aid of another mooring line or by use of the engine. However, it is better to make a practice of not using the engine when approaching the bank, unless the water is clear: you never know what solid objects may be lurking beneath an innocent-looking surface.

Making fast, satisfactorily, requires a meaningful rather

than decorative arrangement of the ropes. Some crews begin
by thinking that the best mooring arrangement must be:

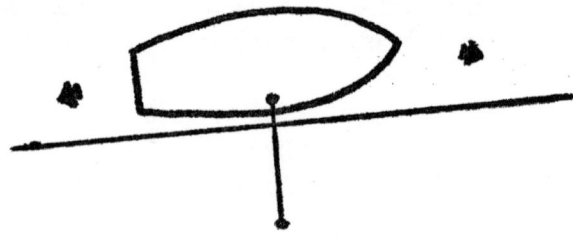

or:

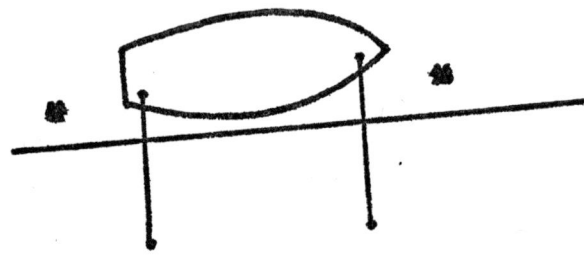

In perfectly still water such an arrangement may suffice but the
wash of passing craft will make the boat move in the directions
arrowed, with consequent buffetings. An improvement is:

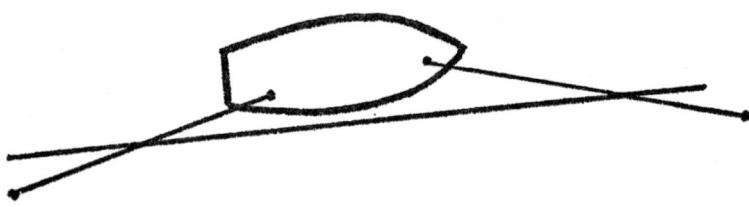

so that any movement is more longitudinal than lateral. A
substantial further improvement is 'springing' which limits
movement much more satisfactorily. Here is an example:

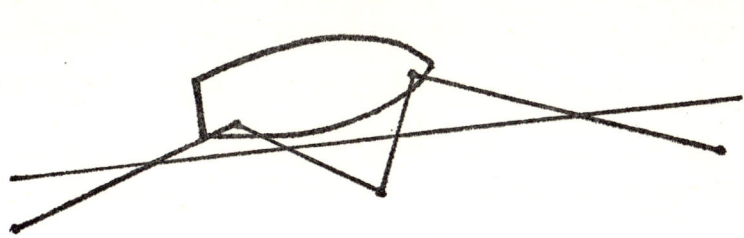

The lines between ship and bank are separate or tied so that they do not slip round the cleats or bollards.

It saves a deal of trouble if each of your mooring lines has a permanently fixed noose at one end: it is a quicker and more convenient method of tying up since there is only one free end to make fast.

Before mooring the boat properly, just peer into the water's edge to see that nothing untoward projects toward the hull. If all is well, ensure that the fenders are so placed that they can do their work between ship and shore. The bollards or rings on French quays are usually arranged for the convenience of 39 metre barges, so you may need plenty of line to secure your boat between two of them. At most town quays though, you will normally find plenty of rings (especially small ones for fishermen's punts). On open banks it may be necessary to drive in pickets. These should be strong and driven in well. They should be angled away from the boat so that the line does not slip off.

Such pickets are almost essential (as well as a sledge hammer for driving them in and knocking them out) for, should you wish to moor on the towpath side of a canal, pickets have to be positioned between the water's edge and the towpath—since it is forbidden (and dangerous) to span the towpath with a rope. You will almost never find bollards here (except just before locks) for, in the days of horse-drawn barges, any boat moored on the towpath side would have been an obstruction, and officially it is still incorrect to moor this side.

WHY LOCKS?

There is absolutely no special skill required to negotiate a lock, however large it may be, but there are several points which, collectively, can ensure a smooth 'locking through'.

First, however, allow me to explain, to those for whom a lock is something new, exactly what it is and how it operates. It is a curious thing that many people have only a hazy idea about the purpose and function of this equipment without which there would be little inland navigation.

The first diagram represents, in exaggerated form, a cross-section of a river running downhill with a shallow depth of water above the bed:

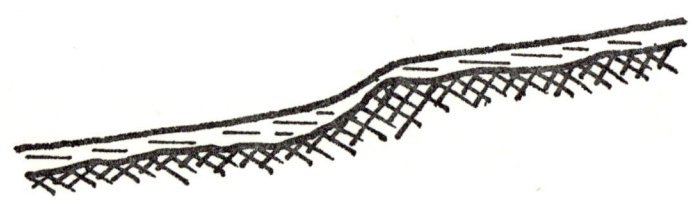

'Canalising' a river ensures the necessary depth of water for navigation. In order to achieve this the slope must be converted into 'steps' with level sections between:

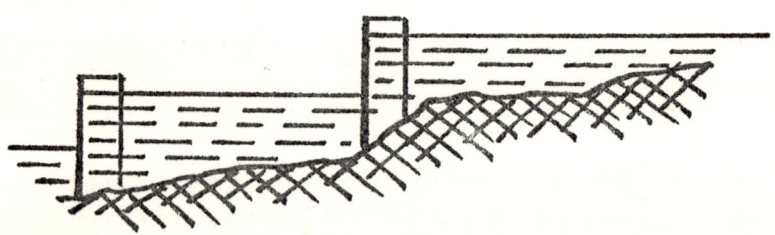

The steps are, in reality, locks or chambers in which the height of the water can be altered so as to raise or lower boats from one level to the other. The only difference between

Page 71 (*left*) The 7-lock staircase at Rogny: commenced in 1605 and abandoned in 1887; (*right*) the last steam tug in France

Page 72 (above) A wedding between two bargee families; (below) the
Palinurus hotel boat

'stepping' a river and a canal is that the bed of the canal between 'steps' or locks is normally level, the canal 'cut' being artificial.

The alteration of boat-level is achieved by a very simple process. Shown below are diagrams of the process for raising and lowering a boat. The diagram shows a two-gate mitre lock (an invention attributed to Leonardo da Vinci) which is typical of French locks.

Boat entering lower gates

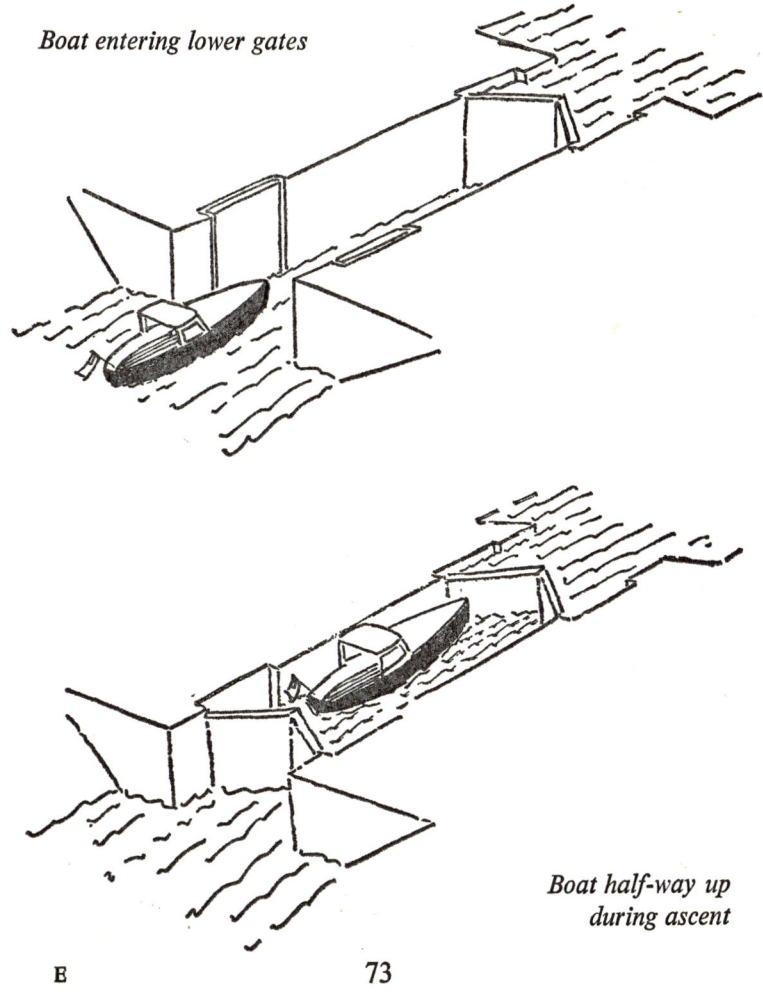

*Boat half-way up
during ascent*

Boat leaving upper gates

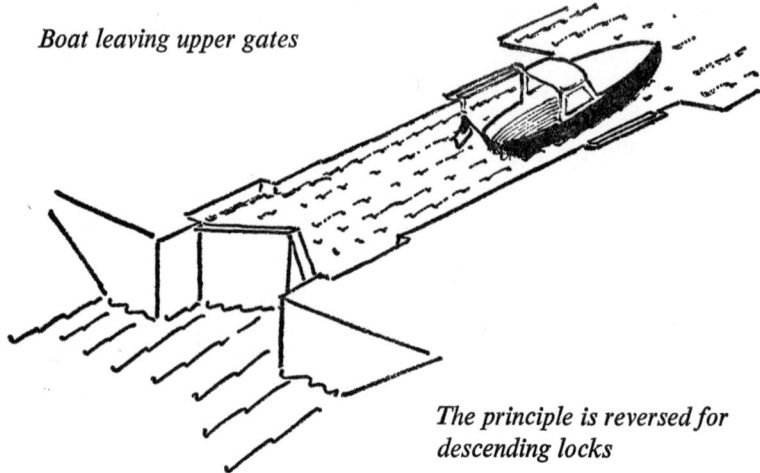

The principle is reversed for descending locks

Now that the principle is established, it will be as well to look at an isometric view of a 'standard' lock and note the features commonly encountered. For the sake of simplicity only one of most of the features referred to are shown on the diagram opposite:

In order to change the water level in a lock, the gates at both ends are closed and a sluice (or paddle)—one or more is contained within each main gate—is opened. In the illustration the sluice (A) is shown open since the water in the lock chamber must have been allowed to escape to permit the opening of the lower gates. (If it were possible to open the lower gate without first letting out the water, the boats in the lock would be swept out in a torrent.) The sluices are raised and lowered by winding handles (or windlasses) (B) and normally you can identify a raised sluice by a length of sluice rack-shaft (or paddle-bar) (C) rising above the gate. The lower gates are then opened by operating the gate rack-and-pinion mechanism (D), of which there is usually one for each gate.

An identical set of gear will be encountered on the far gates. A great variety of winding mechanisms are employed and all look and operate somewhat differently, but the principle is

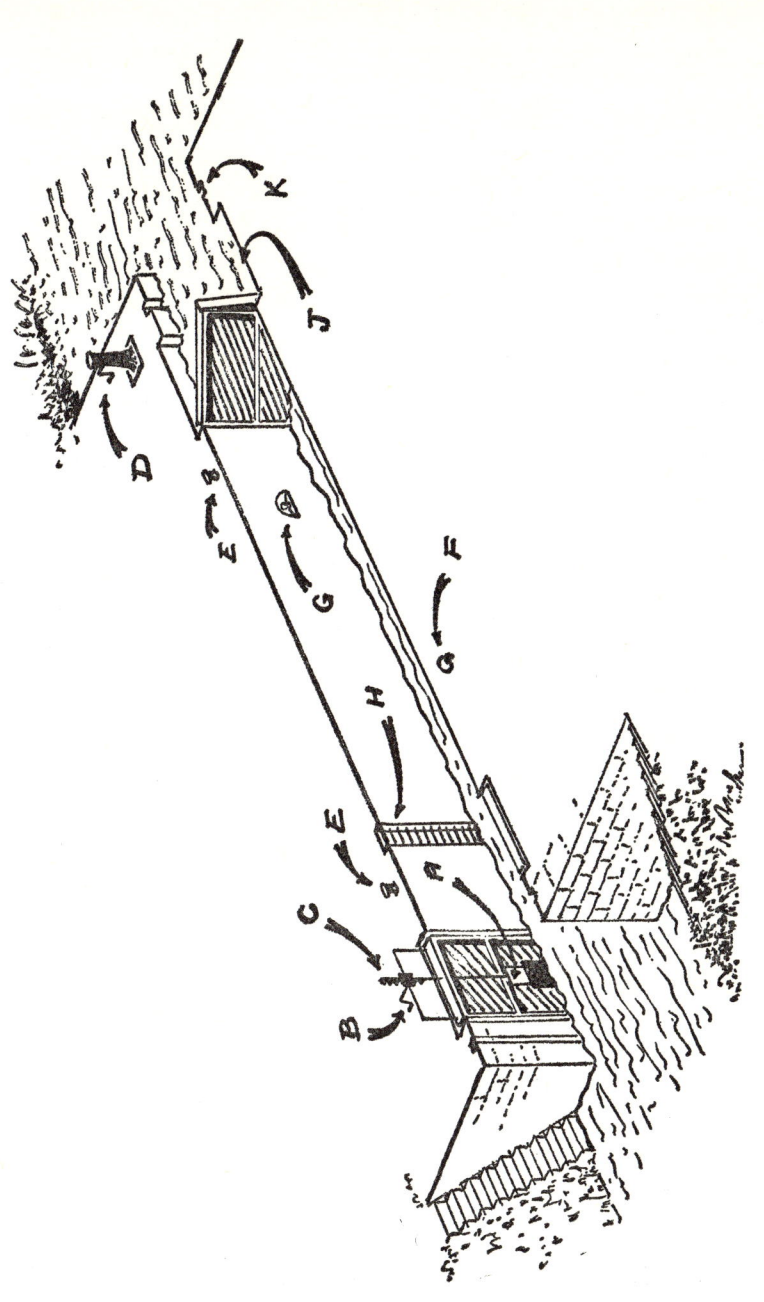

invariable. Water entering the closed chamber raises a boat contained within it and water evacuated lowers it.

The other features illustrated are bollards (E). There are sometimes two, usually four, and on larger locks there may be twenty or more. Or there may be rings (F), but these are less usual. In the taller locks one occasionally encounters small iron bollards set into the wall (G). These conveniently save you climbing the ladder (H) to put a rope round one of the quay-side bollards. (But as the level is raised it is necessary to un-moor and remoor to one of the top bollards and, for reasons noted in the next section, remooring can be undesirable.) Note that when the gates are open, they fit back into a recess (J). The other recess normally incorporated in a lock structure (K) is for fitting a watertight bulkhead across the lock chamber so that it may be pumped dry for repairs.

A feature not shown is a moving or floating bollard, en-countered only in very large locks. This type of bollard is located at deck height. Mounted on a float and contained within a vertical channel, it rises and falls with the vessel and obviates the need for shortening or lengthening the ropes during locking.

The only other feature to note is the sill (or threshold) on to which the upper gates close. It is normally hidden from view by being below water level, even when the lock is at its lowest level. The significance of this from a practical standpoint is that the boat must be positioned so that the bow does not strike it on entering for an ascent nor the stern (or propeller) end up sitting on it in a descent. Sills have spelt doom to some longish craft, so it is as well to keep their existence constantly in mind!

In the busier waterways the sluices and gates are electrically operated. Some of the larger locks have vertical steel shutters instead of mitre gates. It will be seen that with each passage of a boat, whether up or down, a lock-full of water is lost. All canals therefore need to be plentifully supplied with water at their highest level and often at intermediate levels as well.

Where water is short, under conditions of heavy traffic or drought, the 'used' water is sometimes pumped back again into the pound above.

There are one or two other methods in use for raising or lowering boats, but they are very rare. One system admits boats into a large 'box' with removable ends. The box with the boat floating within and the ends closed is raised by a lift or pulled up a slope on rails. The advantage of such a system is to obviate the time needed to negotiate a flight of locks and also to save water. A futuristic scheme involves the use of water slopes in which boats are raised or lowered the length of a steeply inclined channel, a 'pool' of water in which the vessel floats being motivated along the channel by a kind of moving scoop—much on the principle of a grain elevator.

LOCKING THROUGH

Perhaps the easiest way of familiarising oneself with lock procedure is to make an imaginary journey through a lock, rising to the next level.

Any boat ahead of you as you approach has priority, but to avoid waiting pointlessly, keep an eye out to ensure that the boat actually *is* waiting and is not just moored while the crew attend to the week's shopping. In industrial towns barges often draw up in groups waiting for contracts. In any case, barges should not be moored beyond the sign '*Limite de Trématage*' unless they are, in fact, waiting for the lock.

If a commercial barge arrives just after you at a one-barge lock, it is certainly much appreciated—though not expected as a right—if you offer the bargee the chance to go before you. The lock-keeper may be perfectly within his rights—though he will almost certainly not use such powers—if he gives priority to the barge. Obviously if you are pursued by several barges you are not expected to give way to them all!

If you are approaching one of the large remote-controlled locks, on the Seine for example, permission to enter will be signified by a green traffic light (see Chapter Five: 'Rules of the Road'). You may be directed or called forward by a loud-speaker. If you cannot understand, do not despair but keep your eyes open for the hand-signalling of bargees or the lock-keeper which will usually make their intentions quite obvious.

If at your approach the gates are closed, it is customary to give a single blast with the horn (which should be loud if the lock-keeper is to have a chance of hearing it above the noise of water escaping through the lock chamber). It is useful to have field-glasses handy so that you can see if the lock is open or shut from a considerable distance. It is often surprisingly hard to tell. You can then hoot or not as circumstances indicate. If after a decent interval no one stirs, it is best to moor and despatch a member of the crew to investigate.

If you are kept waiting at a lock, do not immediately jump to the conclusion that you are being deliberately neglected. It may be that the lock-keeper has not seen or heard you, that the lock is set for something coming the other way, that there is no one there for a few minutes—some lock-keepers deal with as many as four locks—or the lock-keeper may be feeding the baby, making an omelette or otherwise engaged. Whatever happens, or does not happen, do not attempt to work the lock yourself. It is strictly forbidden and, more significantly, you will certainly incur the hostility of the lock-keeper.

Be patient, especially between noon and 1 pm. This is the hour of the mid-day meal and, although now on some canals the lock-keepers' union has secured a half-hour break for its members, they appreciate being able to have lunch in peace.

Because on most canals the locks are connected to each other by telephone, your impending arrival at the next lock will be known in advance. So, should you decide to stop between locks, you MUST let the lock-keeper know, otherwise the next lock may have been set for you in vain—another boat may appear in the opposite direction and twelve handles have been needlessly turned. You should give warning even though you want to stop for only half an hour. If there is no telephone connection between locks, the lock-keeper will normally ask if you know of any boats following you, so if you do intend to stop, tell the boat ahead if you get the chance.

Normally, as soon as he or she (for many of the lock-keepers are women) has registered your arrival, the lower gates facing you will be opened after the water has been evacuated from the lock-chamber. If your boat is narrow only one of the pair of gates may be opened.

On a standard French canal lock there are twelve operations with a winding handle for the passage of a boat, or twenty-four if the lock has to be reset for a boat following you. It is not only customary, but expected, that help with the winding is given by a crew member. Help with the gates is important for not only are the handles quite exhausting to turn but, if the lock-keeper does not receive help with the second gate, he or she has to walk eighty yards or more round to the other side to deal with it. One seldom encounters a handle *so* heavy that it cannot be turned by a child of, say, nine or ten but for an elderly lock-keeper on a hot day, with many boats to pass through . . . ! And there is nothing like winding handles to promote an appetite and to remove an expanding waist-line. Lock-handles and French food are a perfect balance.

The gate(s) is now open and you enter. Mooring about half-way up the lock chamber, you throw a line to the lock-keeper (or to your crew-member who is already ashore) who places it round a bollard ahead of the bows. The procedure is then repeated for mooring the stern of your boat to a bollard near the end of the lock through which you entered.

It is as well to learn the knack of throwing a line. You should be able to send a noose a good thirty feet with tolerable accuracy. It is a bad start to a new relationship if you strike the lock-keeper or quayside pedestrian with a bundle of wet, tangled rope. And it is not very impressive to watch someone making repeated efforts to throw a dripping line ashore as their boat drifts further and further away. A little practice with the rope, if needed, can be done in the privacy of the countryside before you start! If you fail to master the art you will be better off handing the noose to someone, rather than attempting to throw it. If they are too far away, try putting it on the end of the boat-hook and holding it out.

You need two crew aboard to man the ropes, pulling them in if rising (as in this case) and, of course, letting them out if falling. When descending, a refinement is to pass the rope around the lock-side bollard when mooring—and bringing the end back to the boat again. In this way, when the ascent or descent is finished, you can—by letting go of one end—pull the rope in. It avoids the need to flick the rope off a bollard which, if the lock is deep, can be difficult or impossible.

As shown in the sketch, many locks have a ladder and if not prevented by other traffic, there is something to be said for trying to moor alongside this ladder, especially if you are descending. This makes the ship easily accessible to the lock-side crew at the completion of the manoeuvre. If this is not possible, there is almost always a flight of steps leading to the water's edge at the far end of the lock, beyond the lower gate. Otherwise the crew should re-embark before the descent begins.

If the lock is a large one and you have to share the chamber with a barge, be careful to avoid entering until the barge is properly secured. Otherwise you risk being squashed against the wall while it manoeuvres into position. If you have the choice, it is preferable in a light boat to avoid such sharing, for while a barge is being tied up it may be momentarily drifting and a vessel of 300 tons can squash a fibreglass boat astonishingly flat even though its movement may be almost imperceptible. So don't be in too much of a hurry to enter. But if you have to share, do not be unduly alarmed. A bargee can manoeuvre his vessel to within an accuracy of an inch or so, even with the added difficulty of having you in his way. But be certain that he has seen you.

Once inside you can make fast to the barge's bollards. You then have nothing to worry about as you will be ascending or descending with him and there is no need to lengthen or shorten ropes. Believe it or not, the barge's topsides are likely to be cleaner than those of your boat—even if he is carrying a cargo of coal. For this reason bargees do not appreciate other people walking over their decks.

It is a good idea to keep a bag of sweets handy. Many barges house numerous offspring and sweets offered to the children are enough to promote an extra friendly relationship with a bargee and his wife—with whom, don't forget, you may be spending the day as you progress from lock to lock together. Similarly, cigarettes for the bargee or lock-keeper and—for myself—I keep handy a packet of biscuits for the sad and hungry-looking dogs one sometimes sees chained to a kennel.

Whilst locking through, your fenders should be out as they will be very necessary. Apart from absorbing shocks they will save the sides of the boat from the slime of the lock walls or a barge's side.

Never moor too near either end of the lock. Apart from the danger of the end of your boat becoming caught with the lock-gate, if you are near the forward end when the sluices are opened for an ascent, you may—in a small boat—instantly be flooded.

It is in a lock that you need to be most careful. It is a bad business to fall in. If the sluices are open the turbulence is such that you would be in danger. But if you do have the misfortune to go overboard, swim to the non-turbulent end and hope to find a ladder. Fortunately accidents are rare and when they occur it is usually through carelessness. Wear shoes with rope soles; never leave spare gear lying on the deck where it can trip you up; don't risk a wide jump from ship to shore. And be especially careful when it is wet and slippery.

I repeat, it is best to have a golden rule for children that, if they cannot swim and are too small to help usefully, they should stay below during locking or, if the boat is big enough, be securely harnessed to the deck-centre. At all times they should wear a life-jacket of the new approved design.

As the water is let into the chamber, be prepared for the boat to surge. A light cruiser is easy enough to hold but if attention is wandering and the line allowed to go slack, you may find your craft gathering speed toward one or other lock-gate. If, as the lock-keeper prepares to raise the sluices to admit the water, you are not ready, do not hesitate to signal the fact. A waving of arms is better than a shout because the noise of water and engines will probably drown your voice. For this reason too, it is best to have the lock 'drill' established and rehearsed in advance so that all goes smoothly, without the need for instructions. In the larger locks the movement of the incoming water is sometimes imperceptible. In the smaller ones—which are likely to form the majority—you may at first be awed by the effect of the incoming water cascading violently against your bows. However, as the level rises it becomes more peaceful and as your head rises above the far lock-gate you will find yourself looking at a fresh view from your new elevation: it is extraordinary how a rise of two or three yards offers the inland sailor such a striking change of scene.

If you are secured to a barge, it is best to cast off just before the gates open and secure to a lock-side bollard. Do not economise on effort by neglecting this tying up. As the barge emerges ahead of you, your boat will receive the effect of the thrust of the barge's propeller. Several hundreds of horse power are behind it and you will be unwise to take chances. Similarly, if you are closing a lock gate behind a manoeuvering barge, be careful. It is better to wait until the barge is secured. I have seen the force of water from a churning propeller snatch the handle of the gate-winding mechanism and deliver a bone-breaking blow against its operator. But do not be depressed! Such a circumstance is as rare as it is unnecessary and to be forewarned is, I hope, to ensure that it cannot happen to you.

Do not leave a lock-chamber until the gates are wound back fully into their recesses. Should you bump into, and damage, one which is half-open it could be considered your liability, though to be sure it is your boat that is likely to be damaged, rather than the gate!

When you have been raised to the top, your quayside crew should be ready to help open one of the forward gates. It is polite to take the gate further from the lock-house so that the lock-keeper does not have to walk the extra distance. When descending, the procedure is of course exactly the reverse. The only important thing to remember is to let your lines out steadily as the level descends. Do not, therefore, make a complicated arrangement around your cleats which is liable to jam. If it does, do not try to undo it with your fingers—this is how to lose one—but shout or signal to have the sluices closed. If the warps have not snapped nor the cleat pulled out of the deck, you may need to have some water let back in again to raise the boat and remove the strain on the ropes. If you have a projecting rubbing-strake see that it does not become lodged on the quay-edge as the boat descends.

There are a few locks, mainly on the Seine and Yonne, which have sloping sides instead of vertical walls. Some have one of each, in which case make for the vertical wall. If both sides are sloping and you are descending, you need to be especially careful, the more so if you have a keel which could become lodged on defective masonry. Under these circumstances you must push yourself clear with boat-hooks and for this reason it is a good idea to have two. Because of the possibility of getting 'hung up' in this way, make a rule that nothing is cooking or heating on the stove during lock descents—just in case you find yourself at an angle.

You can now relax and, if your French is up to it, exchange the time of day with the lock-keeper. A few words, or at least smiles, are all that is needed to show friendliness. Tipping is neither required nor expected—except in the area round Paris. But when you have seen great-grandmother struggle with the handles for perhaps the tenth time in the day you may feel that a small *pourboire* is not out of place. For myself, being a believer in tipping only for services rendered, I give between

20 and 50 centimes according to circumstances and the change in my pocket. In the rare event of my encountering a surly lock-keeper I give nothing. The bargees almost always give something; usually 20 centimes.

Every now and again, usually at the main locks, you will be asked to produce your *permis de circulation*. The reason is that the lock-keeper has to record the name of the boat, its tonnage, its destination and the date, in a ledger kept for the purpose. These main locks act also as *poste restante* for the bargees. The lock-keepers at these points are often extraordinarily well-informed about everything to do with the waterways and seemingly most other matters as well.

In a separate breath, but still on the subject of locks, I should mention the existence of *staircase* locks. These have a series of lock-chambers succeeding each other without any pounds between. In staircase locks the procedure is exactly the same as for solitary locks. The gate in front of you becomes the gate behind as you proceed. One possible catch, though! If, when you enter the first chamber in making an ascent, you find that the gates between the first and second chambers are open, you should stop well short of these intermediate gates. This is because the sill of the second chamber may be concealed *just* below water-level and you will risk striking it. These intermediate gates will have been left open as an economy of effort. The double chamber will take twice as long to fill and use twice as much water but none the less, it is a practice often encountered.

I make no apology for having written at length about locks. They are, in reality, simple and they are a source of interest and amusement, the latter chiefly because of the incidental life which surrounds them. But if you know the potential hazards for you, your crew and your boat, you will then be able to enjoy locks secure in the knowledge that they hold no terrors. And let me admit it: at one time or another I think I have committed *all* the errors listed—and I am still alive!

CHAPTER FOUR

General

SHOPPING, WEATHER, CLOTHES AND EATING OUT

Shopping

The cost of living in France is, it is generally agreed, substantially higher than in England but the gap is closing. You will hear people saying that it is as much as 50 per cent higher, and others that there is little in it. The fact is that it is very hard to compare.

At home you know how to shop around; but abroad, because you are new to the place, you tend to miss the bargains. The materials, too, are really not comparable. Meat and vegetables tend to be more expensive in France, weight for weight, but the quality is better (often far better) and consequently there is less waste. Again, there are more street markets in France, and you can often buy relatively cheaply. On some canals the lock-keepers sell their produce (chiefly eggs, honey, vegetables and rabbits) to the bargees.

Food is likely to be by far your greatest expense (leaving out fuel) so you should, in my view, allow perhaps 20 per cent more for the raw materials than for a comparable period in Britain. You will get some of this back on wine—a very drinkable bottle can be yours for 20p! And for your money you should eat better. We have made a practice of taking a box of provisions with us from England. This normally includes some tinned meat, coffee, cereals, good lean bacon and marmalade. The first three as an economy and the others because they are almost unobtainable. Things like candles, soap, tools and hardware are generally all cheaper in England.

Shopping in France is easy. Perhaps it is too easy. A visit to a cheese shop can tempt one into excessive extravagance. If you are on a tight budget you will have to forego many of the mouth-watering delicacies and specialities which you will constantly encounter! Remember that in France most shops close on Mondays, though in a town of any size there is usually one provision shop and one baker open. Even on Sundays and holidays the food shops are normally open in the mornings. On weekdays it is common to find food shops (and many others) open until 8 pm. But almost everything is closed, sealed even, during the sacred lunch hour (sometimes two hours) which starts about mid-day.

Petrol is more expensive than in England. It costs about four times the price of diesel fuel. French cigarettes are less than half price and tobacco almost a quarter. If you are likely to need some proprietary brand of medicine you should bring this with you—the French chemists tend to have their own pharmaceutical favourites. But otherwise you need not lack: if it exists here it is virtually certain to exist there.

Weather

Keeping in mind the remarks made in the section 'Planning Your Cruise' about floods, ice and drought (and the *chômages*), the whole year is cruising-time somewhere in France!

Apart from these rarely-encountered extremes you can enjoy yourself at any season. The country is beautiful in winter and, provided you do not want to sunbathe, you can have excellent journeys 'out of season'. In winter you will, of course, need some form of heating but modern butane gas appliances prevent this being a problem. The only real drawback to winter cruising is the short hours of daylight. Most people will, of course, choose summer. July and August are the French holiday months and the main roads are murderous.

But once you have run the gauntlet (if you are going by car) the waterways are, as usual, almost deserted of pleasure craft. Many of the bargees take their holidays then so it is a good time to go, especially on those waterways which usually have the most traffic.

The centre of France has a marvellous climate in the summer but a colder winter than in England. The southern summers can be very hot—substantially hotter than it ever is in England and the winters are relatively warm. The Brittany region is the most English in weather. There is much less fog than in England but a morning mist often blurs canal and river. Even in the summer when the temperature can easily be 80° F (27° C) or even 90° F (32½° C) in the afternoons, it can still be cool at night.

In the Rhône valley there is the Mistral wind to be considered. It plagues the lower part of the valley and blows with unbelievable ferocity at unpredictable intervals in the summer for periods of three, six or nine days. In the late summer the mosquitoes of the Carmargue are also worth avoiding.

Clothes

Since the climate provides, on the whole, improved English weather, you will need the same sort of clothes. Do not expect *too* much of it though; it can and sometimes does rain. If you bring rubber boots for the wet grass never wear them on a boat—if you fall in they can be most dangerous, especially for children. Casual clothes are fine for all activities although the French tend to be more formally dressed when eating out in the better restaurants, especially for Sunday lunch. All clothes seem to be considerably more expensive in France so don't leave anything behind.

Rope-soled shoes are, in my view, safer than rubber-soled shoes on board. Don't forget sun cream or Vitamin A pills, dark glasses and a sun hat if you are susceptible to the sun's rays: it can burn you quickly on water as the rays are reflected from the surface.

Eating Out

This is expensive. It *can* be ruinous. It will possibly be memorable. If you look at the price of the menus (which are always displayed outside any self-respecting restaurant) and stick to the one of your budget, the only extra apart from service will be the wine—and sometimes even this is included. You can buy excellent meals for £1 per head (including wine) in most towns. Priced 'set' menus are almost always inclusive of service: they usually bear the words *'service compris'* ('service included') or the letters S.T.C. ('Service and taxes included'). But with a family or large crew, the pounds soon mount up and, sad though it is, the beginning of economy in France is to eat at home. But a cruise without a visit to a restaurant would be a cheerless event. So choose carefully and enjoy it! French families tend to make an occasion of Sunday lunch at a restaurant so it is a meal to avoid having out—the prices and service both suffer.

There are numerous guide books to the restaurants of France. At one time or another I have tried most of the better known ones but every time I return to the *Guide Michelin*, most famous of them all. It is astonishingly accurate—that is to say, it seems to be right about nine times out of ten, which is a very high average. But it does not list the cheapest restaurants or small cafés—many of which are excellent value for money—which is a great pity. However, there are a number of publications which attempt to rectify this omission; amongst the best known is the *Relais Routiers*.

COMMERCIAL TRAFFIC

It may be of interest to know what kind of 'competition' exists on the waterways.

Apart from the thin sprinkling of pleasure craft and some 500 assorted 'oddities', there are just over 1,200 river freighters and 5,500 canal barges, mainly of the 250–300 ton variety.

Page 89 (*above*) Sad end to a long life; (*below*) a hire cruiser on the Nivernais

Page 90 (*above*) A sharp bend in a narrow canal; (*below*) Canal de l'Est
beneath the slopes of the Ardennes

These barges, which are normally 38½m (126ft) long, are the 'standard' canal craft and in a variety of forms are to be seen everywhere. They have accommodation aft for the skipper and his family and sometimes separate accommodation in the fo'c'sle for a 'hand'. Unladen, they loom above you and seem to occupy the whole width of the canal cut. Laden, they have sometimes only a few inches of freeboard and it seems that the slightest wash will sink them. About 80 per cent of these barges are skipper-owned and they provide a modest living for their crew. However curious you may be to see the inside of one of these barges, it is absolutely not done to peer in through the portholes. Bargees have a small enough area of privacy and value what they have. Equally they would not dream of trespassing on yours.

If you have problems of a marine nature, these are the people whose help you need. It will be given unstintingly and cheerfully with apparently no regard to their tight schedule. A glass of wine or a pot of English marmalade makes a more acceptable present than money.

On the larger rivers, where the locks are longer, the commercial viability of these barges is increased by forming a double unit, end to end, in which the forward vessel is pushed by the one behind. Being completely secured together the unit acts as a single barge of 77m (252ft 7in) length and operates with only one set of crew. Occasionally this unit is formed in a side-to-side arrangement. There are over 800 such 'pushed' barges. However, you will also see two separate barges, both with engines running, lashed together in this manner. This is for the social opportunity it offers and the additional relaxation of one of the skippers.

Again, where the locks are large enough to permit it, there are 'pushers' operating. Generally these are modern craft designed to push (rather than tow) trains of two, four, six or even eight barges (or lighters), two abreast. Some of the smaller pushers are used only by day and have no accommodation; others have all the room and amenities of a four-bedroomed

F   91

house. Such pushers may be employed also to move huge barges (or floating tanks as they are also known) and these can have a capacity of up to 2,000 tons. You will of course encounter these only where the locks are of the largest dimensions.

There are also a number of tankers which vary from small ones of 200 tons (used mainly for wine) on the *Canal du Midi* to the 1,000 tonners on the Seine.

Above such a capacity most of the shipping tends to be seagoing and consequently confined to the estuarial seaways, such as the Seine as far as Rouen, the Loire as far as Nantes, the Charente as far as Tonnay-Charente, the Gironde as far as Bordeaux, and the Adour as far as Bayonne.

Of commercial craft smaller than the 'standard' barge there remains little evidence.

You may see an occasional tug—descendant of the old steam tugs which used to haul trains of barges up-river—but it will probably only be commuting with a sand-laden lighter between dredgers and riverside sand-heaps. The dredgers themselves, though static, deserve a mention through sheer weight of numbers. They are frequently encountered on the bigger rivers and whilst of themselves they cause little or no hazard to navigation, the steel hawsers which secure them to the river bank can be a source of danger. The theory is that as you approach you hoot—and the cables are then temporarily unwinched to allow you to sail over them. But in reality the noise of the dredging machinery is so great that the crew often fail to hear you—so it is best to wait until you see the winch being lowered. The cables themselves are not always easy to see and are sometimes just below the surface. Make sure you pass the dredgers on the side indicated by the red and white signals.

In most ports and before many locks you will see the maintenance pontoons of the *Ponts et Chaussées*, equipped with a variety of gear according to the many functions they are there to perform.

BATHING

The canals are often a great deal less adulterated than they appear: owing to their shallowness the passing traffic stirs the sediment and clouds the water. Canals in many cases take their water from a mountain lake brought over great distances by feeder streams or aqueducts and are often cleaner than rivers which, being at the lowest level, receive the most drainage.

You need to use your judgement about bathing. A look at the map gives the best idea about possible sources of contamination. Anyway, too lively an imagination about the possible constituents of the liquid can ruin your bathing. I have bathed in any number of the quieter canals and rivers, as have thousands of Frenchmen, and have survived apparently unscathed. But in this age of mass pollution where even the sea is contaminated, it must be wisest not to gulp large quantities of water. Certainly to bathe in the lower reaches of the large rivers would be highly dangerous—as in Britain, the chemical effluent is shocking.

When river bathing, keep a good eye out for weed. It can get caught around your legs and then—if you panic—you can wind yourself to the bottom. And of course, the common-sense rules apply: never dive in without having first checked for weed and for adequate depth. Make sure there is somewhere you can get out easily. Do not swim in rivers with a swift current. Watch out for traffic. Never let small children swim without constant supervision nor without a life-jacket unless they are exceptionally proficient.

FISHERMEN AND FISHING

The fishermen you encounter are likely to be pursuing their hobby with a passionate seriousness. Since even the slow passage of your boat does nothing to improve their chances of success, you may see one or two dejected or even grim faces turned your way. But it is wrong to take this amiss. Most fishermen are outstandingly friendly and patient and will happily return your salutation. More than once have we been given a share of the day's catch. They are a cross-section of the country's inhabitants. In July or August they are usually enjoying their holiday and probably come from opposite corners of France. The motionless figure in blue denim and wide straw hat may be a candlestick maker from Marseilles or, equally well, a Director of the Credit Lyonnais in Lille.

Already there when the mist rises in the morning, you will see the fishermen fading into obscurity as night descends. It is as well to give audible warning of your approach, especially round canal corners. A bargee will not hear you but it will give a fisherman with three lines out a little time to take precautions. If you suddenly appear, bearing down on his equipment, he may panic and use words not taught to him by his mother.

If you too want to fish this is easy to arrange. So, if you are a fishing enthusiast, don't forget to bring your rod. The procedure is this:

What the Law Requires: The angler, before fishing, must each year:
1. Be a member of an angling and fish-breeding association (an *'association de pêche et de pisciculture'*, or *'APP'*) of his choice, and approved by the regional Prefect. On paying his annual subscription (rate of which varies from one association to another), the angler receives a membership card in his name (and only for his personal use).
2. Pay for the fish-breeding tax-stamps. According to the kind of fishing practised (ground-bait fishing; spinning) or the kind of fish sought (salmon), the angler has one or more of the following tax-stamps affixed to his *APP* membership card:
    (a) obligatory, the *'pêche au coup'* (ground-bait fishing) stamp;
    (b) optional, and supplementary to (a), the *'lancer'* (spinning) stamp;

(c) optional, and supplementary to (a) and (b), the '*saumon*' (salmon) stamp;

(d) if occasion arises, and supplementary to (a), the '*diman-ches et jours fériés*' (Sundays and general holidays) stamp. The last-named permits fishing on Sundays and general holidays during the general close season, in waters of the second category (coarse fish predominating), and only in certain counties of France (apply for information to the angling and fish-breeding associations).

(The proceeds of taxes paid by anglers are remitted, through the county federations of the angling and fish-breeding associations, to the '*Conseil Supérieur de la Pêche*', an organisation responsible, under the '*Eaux et Forêts*' and the '*Ponts et Chaussées*' Departments, for the expense of supervising and maintaining the fish-breeding areas.)

NB—*Cards and stamps are issued:*

1. By the anglers' associations.
2. By most of the fishing-tackle dealers delegated by the associations.

Classification of Waterways
There are two categories of waterways, lakes and pools, according to the varieties of fish predominating in them, and to the ownership of the waterways, etc.

(a) First-category waterways: those with trout.
(b) Second-category waterways: those with coarse fish.
Public waterways: fishing rights belong to the State.
Private waterways: fishing rights belong to a private owner, to an association, or to a commune.

Close Season
1. *General restrictions*
To facilitate fish-breeding, the general close periods for angling are fixed according to categories of waterways as follows:
First category: from last Tuesday in September to third

Friday in February, except in the following counties:

(a) Côtes-du-Nord, Finistère, Ille et Vilaine, Manche and Morbihan (closure from second Tuesday in September to third Friday in February);

(b) Hautes-Alpes, Isère, Savoie and Haute-Savoie (closure from second Tuesday in October to third Friday in February);

(c) Eure, Nord, Pas-de-Calais, Seine-Maritime and Somme (closure from first Tuesday in October to last Friday in March).

Second category: from Tuesday following 15 April to Friday following 15 June.

NB—These periods apply to all fish except salmon (see following paragraphs). Migratory fish: alose, bass, flounder, mullet, can be fished for in certain counties during the general close season (apply locally for information).

2. *Particular restrictions*

Outside the general close periods, angling for the following is not allowed:

First-category rivers:

Gudgeon from Tuesday following 15 April to Friday following 15 June

Chub All the year.

Grayling from 1 March to 14 May. Nevertheless, fishing for grayling, with fly only and a maximum of two hooks per line, is allowed in certain rivers up to 31 December.

Second-category rivers:

Pike from 1 February to 31 March or, in certain counties, till Tuesday following 15 April.

Grayling from 1 January to Friday following 15 June.

Salmon the periods of general closure (First and Second categories) do not apply to this species. Special restrictions exist in both categories of waterways, varying according to the counties. Apply for information locally.

3. *Preserves*

Preserves are created to ensure maintenance of stocks. They are indicated by notices. Fishing at these spots is barred at all times.

Regulations During the Fishing Seasons
1. *Public waterways or lakes*

With only one floating or spinning line (spinning is with a floating line) the angler possessing a card with tax-stamps may fish freely.

With more than one floating line (maximum permit is for three floating lines) he may fish only on stretches controlled by the association to which he belongs. If he wishes to fish with two or three floating lines on a stretch of public property other than that of the association whose card he holds, he must join the *APP* which holds the fishing rights. The angler pays the cost of the new card, but not of the further tax-stamps.

On all the stretches controlled by the association or associations of which he holds cards, the angler must observe the regulations of the associations, which are generally printed on the cards.

2. *Private waterways*

To fish in private waterways anglers must apply for authorisation to the holder of the fishing rights (riparian proprietor, commune, or association). This written authorisation is indispensable; it may involve a fee, or not.

3. *Fishing hours*

During the angling periods, fishing is authorised from half an hour before sunrise to half an hour after sunset.

4. *Sizes of fish*

Anglers must return undersized fish to the water.

5. *Special regulations*

Certain departures from the general rules are accorded by the Prefects. To prevent involuntary infringement of rules and consequent bother with the authorities, tourist anglers should apply for information in the locality:

at Town Halls ('*Mairies*') where Prefectorial orders (standing rules and annual notices) are posted up;

to the county federations of fishing and fish-breeding
associations;

to the local *Associations de Pêche et de Pisciculture* (*APP*);

to periodicals dealing with angling;

to retailers of fishing tackle.

(This last is likely to be the simplest and most practical source
of information.)

Remember, though, it is forbidden to fish within fifty metres
of a lock or where you see the sign *Pêche Gardée*.

Rules of the Road

The following is a simplified list of rules which are applicable on the French waterways. Their enforcement is in small evidence and you are most unlikely to be pursued should you be in default on some minor point. However, there is a good reason for the rules having been established, although the logic behind some of them may only become evident as you gather experience.

Their particular significance is that, in the unhappy event of an accident, the rule book will certainly be applied and, as with the 'Highway Code' on British roads, it is well worth being closely familiar with the contents.

Under the section entitled 'Permits' in Chapter Two I have already listed the paperwork required.

1. Boats must be seaworthy and not overloaded. Visibility from the helmsman's seat must be unobstructed.
2. The following equipment is obligatory for vessels of less than 10 tons:
   An audible signal capable of being heard at 500 metres; 2 life belts; boat-hook; mooring ropes; first-aid box; anchor (whilst in rivers); 2 oars; fire extinguisher.
3. In addition, it is recommended that each passenger should have a life-jacket, and that each boat should carry:
   a bailer; a red flag and a blue flag (required on certain rivers, principally the Seine).
4. Navigation lights are only required for navigation at night or whilst being stationed in a waterway used at night. For

boats of less than 12 metres length, standard equipment usually provided (sometimes as an extra) on British-made cruisers is sufficient.

5. Boats must be marked with their name and port of registration.
6. The engine fuel tanks and gas cylinders must be so arranged as to avoid any risk of explosion. If these tanks are situated on deck, they must be secured in such a way that it is impossible for them to fall over. They must also be protected from sun and risk in a collison.
7. A metal container should be placed beneath the engine so as to catch and contain any leaks of oil or petrol, to prevent their flowing into the bilges.
8. For engines of more than 10hp fitted to a boat weighing less than 800kg, there should be a security device which cuts the electrical or fuel supply in the event of the driver being ejected.
9. Pleasure boats are free to navigate only if they do not impede commercial navigation. (There are complex regulations concerning the degree of priorities—or lack of them—for pleasure craft in the passage of locks, according to the various regions travelled. For instance, the right to pass through a lock solo—that is, without a commercial barge—may not exist. Since the rules relating to this are voluminous I think it sufficient to say that, having myself passed through almost all the canals and rivers mentioned in this book, I have never had to wait for commercial traffic for this reason. Nevertheless, it is an additional reason, if one is needed, to remain on friendly terms with the agents of the navigational service and, in the unlikely event of a dispute, it would be as well to check the rules pertaining to navigation on the river or canal concerned.)
10. You may not moor or anchor in the navigable channel.
11. Your boat must keep a sufficient distance from other boats, whether moored or in passage, so as to avoid risk of collision.

12. There is a speed limit on all waterways—see Appendix A: 'Speed Limits'.
13. In times of fog it is not permitted to navigate unless you can see a distance of at least 300m.
14. Unless otherwise indicated by signs situated on the bank, the right half of the channel is reserved for traffic going in your direction.
15. When crossing, both boats should slow down.
16. If there is insufficient room to permit a crossing, the boat going upstream should pull in to the side, giving priority to the boat heading downstream. Note: In canals, upstream is climbing and downstream is descending the slope.
17. In tidal reaches the boat travelling with the tide has priority.
18. On certain rivers, such as the Rhine, Moselle, Lower Seine and Rhône, a blue flag (approximately 2ft × 3ft on a stick 5ft long) is held out on the side of the boat which is to pass a vessel going in the opposite direction. This rule applies only if the boat going upstream wishes to hold to the left side instead of the right. In this case he will hold a blue flag out to starboard, as will the oncoming (downstream) boat to show that the signal has been understood. At night the blue flag is replaced by a flashing white light. A red flag of similar dimensions is held out to indicate a turn to be made in that direction.
19. If you encounter a boat being *hauled* towards you from the towpath on your side you must pass to the left of it.
20. On lakes and open water the normal sea rule applies: that is to say, when two boats are approaching each other, to avoid collision both steer to starboard. Similarly, if the possibility of a collision is envisaged between two boats on convergent courses, the vessel on your right has priority, so you need to steer to starboard to avoid it.

    The two foregoing rules apply to craft of similar status. In the case of the other craft being a passenger boat, police boat or sailing boat, you must give way.
21. In overtaking, pass the overtaken vessel on the left.

Similarly, if you are being overtaken, maintain your course on the right. An exception to this last rule will arise when the boat to be overtaken is being hauled from the left bank.

22. When being overtaken, slow down so that the overtaking process is made as short as possible.

23. Overtaking is forbidden:
    (i) where shown by appropriate signs on the bank;
    (ii) throughout narrow passages;
    (iii) under bridges;
    (iv) beyond the signs *limite de trematage* which will be encountered before each lock.

24. You should be familiar with the code of sound signals (see Nos 38–43 on pages 103 and 104).

25. According to signals, permission may need to be obtained before passing through a tunnel.

26. When mooring before a lock, the position of your boat must be such that it in no way impedes any boats which emerge from the lock.

27. Boat crews may help lock-keepers with their work but must abide by the lock-keeper's instructions.

28. Water-skiing may only be practised in the areas of river or lake set aside for the purpose.

29. You may not stop in a lock for a greater time than is necessary for the actual locking.

30. You may not moor in a narrow passage, on the immediate approach to a lock, opposite ferry crossing points, nor before public wash-houses. Nor may a mooring rope be attached to trees, electric or telephone poles, kilometric posts, signposts, seats or any other object not intended for the purpose. A mooring rope must not stretch across a navigable channel, nor across the arch of a bridge, nor across the towpath.

31. It is forbidden to drive any vehicle, including a bicycle, along the towpath. (This rule is not strictly observed in so far as bicycles are concerned.)

32. In order to leave a boat moored for a long duration, you need to comply with special conditions (which are dealt with under a separate heading).
33. It is forbidden to throw rubbish on to the canal or river banks.
34. You are not allowed to work any lock or mobile bridge without the authority of the lock- or bridge-keeper.
35. You walk at your own risk on all 'works'.
36. In the event of an accident you must inform the nearest agent of the navigation service.
37. If you are navigating during times of flood, you must keep in touch with the *Service d'Annonce des Crues* of the *Ponts et Chaussées*.
38. Sound signals are composed of long and short blasts. A long blast (–) should have a duration of four seconds. A short blast (.) should have a duration of one second. The interval between the two blasts should be one second.

-	Attention
..	I am going to port
.	I am going to starboard
...	I am going astern
....	I am unable to manoeuvre
....	(continuous series of short blasts) Imminent danger of collision
- - -	(repeated at intervals) Distress sign.

39. When using these signals for crossing or overtaking, the other vessel should answer with the appropriate sound signals. (For example, in the event of crossing a boat on the abnormal, or left side, you would sound two short blasts to indicate that you are keeping to the left and should receive a reply of two short blasts to indicate that the other boat is keeping to its left. If, however, you receive in reply one short blast, you should cross to the other side as it will indicate that the other vessel intends to remain on your left side.)
40. The following signals are used for overtaking:

- - .	I wish to overtake on your starboard
- - ..	I wish to overtake on your port
	(as for crossing, the other boat should reply with one or two short blasts indicating agreement or disagreement)
	If, in reply, you receive:
.....	(5 short blasts) this indicates that you must NOT overtake.

41. The sound signals for turning are:

- .	I am going to turn to starboard
- ..	I am going to turn to port.

42. There are sound signals where a boat is to emerge at a waterway junction:

- - - .	I am going to turn to starboard
- - - ..	I am going to turn to port
- - -	I am going straight across.

43. Sound signals which should be used in crowded waterways which are fogbound are: one long blast repeated each minute for any boat still under way (two long blasts are used by convoys); boats (or dredgers) which are stopped in the navigable channel will sound bells: a single peal indicates a free passage to the left side of the channel and a double peal for the right side.

Glossary of Useful Phrases

Where may I buy petrol/diesel oil/provisions?
Où puis-je acheter de l'essence/du gazoil/des comestibles?

Where may I obtain water?
Où puis-je trouver de l'eau?

Do you have a hose?
Avez-vous un tuyeau pour amener l'eau?

Where is the lock-keeper?
Où est Monsieur l'éclusier?

At what time does the lock open?
A quelle heure l'écluse sera-t-elle ouverte?

To wind a lock sluice handle.
Faire tourner une manche de la vanne (porte d'écluse).

Which side is the towpath?
Le chemin de halage se trouve de quel côté?

May I moor here?
Est-ce qu'on peut amarrer ici?

Are there any obstacles in the next pound/reach?
Est-ce qu'il existe des obstacles au cours du prochain bief?

Are there any barges coming?
Est-ce qu'il y a des péniches qui viennent?

I wish to stop for the night in the next pound/reach.
J'aimerais passer la nuit dans le prochain bief.

I shall be starting at . . . o'clock tomorrow.
Je partirai demain vers . . . heures.

Can you direct me to a good mechanic?
Connaîssez-vous un bon mécanicien?

Please take this line and make it fast.
Prenez cette corde, s'il vous plaît, et l'attachez.

Where can I obtain gas refills?
Ou est-ce qu'on peut trouver des rechanges de gaz?

Is this water fit for drinking?
Est-ce que c'est de l'eau potable?

Is it dangerous to swim here?
Est-ce qu'il est dangereux de se baigner ici?

Where can I get a fishing licence?
Ou puis-je obtenir un permis de pêche?

May I fish here?
Est-ce qu'il est permis de pêcher ici?

Please let the water in slowly.
Faites entrer l'eau doucement, s'il vous plaît.

How far is it to the next lock?
La prochaine écluse est à quelle distance?

How long will it take to mend?
La réparation prendra combien de temps?

What is the name of this village/town?
Comment s'appelle ce village/cette ville?

Is it permitted to water ski here?
Est-ce qu'on peut faire du ski-nautique ici?

Where can I obtain the services of a pilot?
Où puis-je trouver un pilote?

Under which arch of the bridge is the channel?
Sous quel arche du pont se trouve le chenal?

What is the minimum depth in the next reach/pound?
Quelle est la profondeur du prochain bief au plus bas?

Page 107 (*above*) A reach of the lower Rhône; (*below*) *Le Pont d'Avignon*

Page 108 (*above*) Sunset over the Seine; (*below*) canal deep in leaf

Glossary of Words

acid	acide
alongside	bord à bord
to come alongside	accoster
anchor	ancre (f)
anchorage	mouillage (m)
astern (to go)	marcher en arrière
auger	tarière (f)
backwash	remous (m)
bailer	épuisette, écope (f)
bakery	boulangerie (f)
ball-bearing	roulement à filles (m)
ball-thrust	roulement de butée
bank (of river)	rive (f)
(of canal)	berge (f)
barge	péniche (f) chaland (m)
bargee	marinier (m)
battery (top up)	batterie (niveau d'eau)
beacon	balise (f)
beam (breadth of)	largeur (f)
bearing (of machine)	palier (m)
ball-bearing	palier à billes
thrust bearing	palier butée
belay	amarrer
bilge	cale (f)
block	poulie (f)
single block	poulie simple
double block	poulie double
snatch block	poulie coupée
boat-hook	gaffe (f)
bollard	bitte (f) bollard (m)
bore (river)	mascaret (m) ras de marée (m)

G

109

English–French

bolt	boulon
bottom	fond (m)
flat-bottomed	à fond-plat
bow	avant (m)
on the port bow	par babord avant
brace	vilebrequin à cliquet
bradawl	poinçon (m)
brass	laiton (m)
bridge (carrying canal)	pont-canal (m)
bulkhead	cloison (f)
watertight bulkhead	cloison étanché
buoy	bouée (f)
mooring-buoy	bouée de corps morts
buoy-rope	orin (m)
burgee	guidon (m)
bush (of machine)	manchon (m)
butcher	boucherie (f)
camshaft	arbre à cames
capsize	chavirer
carburettor	carburateur
carburettor (needle)	pointeau (m)
float	flotteur (m)
jet	jicleur (m)
careen	caréner
careening-basin	bassin de carénage
caulk	calfater
caulking	calfatage (m)
centre-punch	pointeau (m)
channel (connecting salt lake to sea)	grau (m)
chemist	pharmacien (m)
circulatory pump	pompe de circulation
cleat	taquet (m)
clinker	clin (m)
clinker-built	construit à clin
close, shut (canal)	chômage (m)
coamings	hiloire (f) surbau (m)
collar (machine)	machon (m)
confluence (rivers)	confluent (m)
connecting-rod	bielle (f)
contact-breaker	rupteur (m) interrupteur
contact-breaker arm	levier du rupteur
contact-point	plot (m)
cork	liège (m)

Glossary of Words

cradle (for vessel)	berceau (m)
launching cradle	ber (m)
crankshaft	vilebrequin (m)
cruising permit	permit de circulation
cylinder	cylindre (m)
diesel oil	mazout, gasoil, fuel
dike	digue (f)
distributor	distributeur
distributor head	distributeur de courant
diver	scaphandrier (m)
dock (no gates)	darse (f)
downstream	aval
draught (of vessels)	calaison (f) tirant d'eau
drill	mèche (f)
hand-drill	chignole (f)
drinking water	l'eau potable
dynamo	dynamo
eddy	remous (m)
engine	moteur
eyelet (canvas)	oeil de pie (m)
fairlead	chaumard (m)
fan belt	courroie (f)
fast (to make)	amarrer
ferry	bac (m)
fid	epissoir (m)
figure of eight (knot)	noeud d'arret (m)
file	rame (f)
fill up	faire le plein
filter	pessoire (f) filtre (f)
fire extinguisher	extincteur (m)
firing order (motor)	ordre d'allumage (f)
first-aid box	boîte de premier secours
fish	pêcher
fisherman	pêcheur
fishmonger	poissonnerie (f)
fit out	équiper
flag	drapeau (m) pavillon
flukes (of anchor)	pattes (f)
four-stroke motor	moteur à quatre temps
frogman	homme grenouille
fuel tank	réservoir d'essence/gasoil
gas refills	recharge de gaz

gland (stuffing)	presse étoupe (m)
grocer	epicerie (f)
halliard	drisse (f)
hammer	marteau (m)
hardware shop	quincaillerie
heart (of rope)	mèche (f)
hitch (rolling)	noeud de fouet (m)
clove hitch	deux demi-clefs à capeler
half-hitch	demi-clef
timber hitch	noeud de bois
Blackwall hitch	gueule de loup
horn	signal sonore
hose	tuyau flexible (m)
insulation tape	chatterton (m)
injector	injecteur
ironmongers	quincaillerie (f)
jointing compound	hermétic (m
knot	noeud
figure-of-eight	noeud d'arret
granny	noeud de vache
bowline	noeud de chaise
running bowline	noeud d'anguille
reef	noeud de plat
fisherman's bend	noeud de grapplin
sheet bend	noeud d'écoute
ladder	échelle (f)
lay up	désarmer
leak	voie d'eau
spring a leak	faire une voie d'eau
stop a leak	aveugler une voie d'eau
left bank	rive gauche
life-belt	ceinture de sauvetage
lifebuoy	bouée de sauvetage
life-jacket	gilet de sauvetage
lights (navigation)	feux de route
riding light	feu de position
masthead light	fanal (m)
lock	écluse (f)
lock sill	busc (m)
lock-keeper	éclusier

lock—*cont.*	écluse (f)
lock sluice handle	manivelle (f)
to lock through	sasser
lock chamber	sas (m)
list, heel (of boat)	bande, gite
to have a list	avoir de la bande, avoir de la gite
meeting (in a river)	croisement (m)
methylated spirit	alcool à brûler
misfire (motor)	avoir des ratées
moor	mouiller
mooring	amarrage (m)
mooring buoy	bouée de corps mort
mooring ring	boucle (f) anneau (m)
mop	guipon (m)
mould	gabarit (m)
moulding	lisse (f)
nail	clou (m)
narrow passage	passage rétréci
nut	écrou
wing nut	papillon (m)
oar	aviron (m) rame (f)
oil	huile (f)
oil-grooves	pattes d'araignée (f)
oil-level	niveau d'huile
outboard	moteur hors-bord
overtake	dépasser
overtaking (in river)	trématage
no overtaking	limite de trématage
painter (of boat)	bosse (f)
paraffin	pétrole (superieur) (m)
pennant	guidon (m)
petrol	essence (f)
petrol pump	pompe en essence
petrol tank	reservoir à essence
picket/stake	piquet (m)
pilot	pilote (m)
pin (machine)	goupille (f)
split-pin	goupille fendue
pine	pin (m)
pitch pine	pitch-pin (m)
piston	piston (m)

English–French

pitch (tar)	brai (m)
pitch (of a screw)	pas (m)
plane (for wood)	rabot (m)
pliers	pince (f)
plywood	contre-plaqué (m)
port	babord
'pound' of canal	bief (m)
pricker	poincon (m)
propeller	hélice (f)
pitch of a propeller	pas de l'hélice
propeller shaft	arbre d'hélice
pump	pompe (f)
bilge pump	pompe de cale
circulatory pump	pompe de circulation
to prime a pump	allumer une pompe
pump water from a boat	agrèner
rabbet	râblure (f)
radiator	radiateur (m)
raft	radeau (m)
reach (of a canal)	bief (m)
ream (to ream a hole)	fraiser
red lead	minium (m)
reduction gear	réducteur
right bank	rive droite
ring (mooring)	anneau (m)
rising water (river)	hausse (f)
rope	cordage (m)
hemp rope	cordage en chanvre
rowlocks	dames de uage (f)
rubbing strake	lisse (f)
rudder	gouvernail (m)
sailor (at sea)	marin
sailor (inland), bargee	marinier
screw	vis, hélice (f)
screw (thread)	visser
screwdriver	tournevis
screw up	serrer
unscrew	dévisser, déserrer
scupper	dalot (m)
self-starter	démarreur
shackle	manille (f)
shaft	arbre
cam-shaft	arbre à cames

shaft—*cont.*	arbre
crankshaft	vilebrequin (m)
propeller shaft	arbre d'hélice
shallows	haut-fonds (m)
shoals	haut-fonds, bas-fonds (m)
ship's chandler	magasin pour articles de marine
sill (of a lock)	busc (m)
sledgehammer	marteau de forgeron
sling (to)	élinguer
slipway	cale (f)
sluice	vanne (f)
solder	souder
soft-solder	souder à l'etain
spanner	clé (f)
adjustable spanner	clé à molette
sparking-plug	bougie
splice	épisser
eye-splice	épissure à oeil
spring washer	rondelle à ressort, rondelle grover
stanchion	montant (m), rembard de protection
starboard	tribord
starter (motor)	démarreur (m)
strainer	crépine, passoire (f)
strand (of a rope)	tournon (m)
stringer	lisse (f)
stuffing box	presse-étoupe (f)
switch (electrical)	interrupteur (m)
tap	robinet (m)
tar (coal)	goudron (m)
tarpaulin	prelart (m), bâche goudronnée (f)
tow (by boat)	remorquer
towage	halage (m)
tow-path	chemin de halage
training wall (river)	digue, épine (f)
tributary	affluent (m)
tug-boat	remorqueur (m)
tunnel	souterrain (m)
turn (of a rope)	tour
a round turn	un tour mort
turn (or turning)	virement (m)
turn a boat	virer
twine	fil (m)
sail twine	fil à voile

English–French

underwriter	assureur (m)
unmoor	larguer
upstream	amont
valve	valve, soupape
wash (of a boat)	remous (m)
washer	rondelle (f)
watershed	versant (m)
water cock	vanne de prise d'eau (f)
water ski	ski nautique (m)
water tank	reservoir à eau (f)
weir	barrage (m) déversoir (m)
weld	souder à l'autogene
wing nut	papillon (m)
whip (a rope)	surlier
whipping	serliure (m)
wire (metal)	fil (m)
brass wire	fil de laiton (m)
copper wire	fil de cuivre rouge (m)
ignition wire	fil de bougie (m)
iron wire	fil de fer (m)

Glossary of Words

French–English

bitte (f)	bollard
boîte de premier secours	first-aid box
bosse (f)	painter (of a boat)
boucherie (f)	butcher
boucle (f)	mooring ring
bouée (f)	buoy
bouée de sauvetage	lifebuoy
orin (m)	buoy rope
bougie	sparking plug
boulangerie (f)	bakery
boulon	bolt
busc (m)	sill (of a lock)
cale (f)	slipway, bilge
calfater	to caulk
carburateur	carburettor
caréner	to careen
bassin de carénage	basin for careening
chatterton (m)	insulation tape
ceinture de sauvetage	lifebelt
chaland (m)	lighter, barge
chaumard (m)	fairlead
chavirer	capsize
chemin de halage	towpath
chignole (f)	hand-drill
chomâge (m)	closing or shutting down, stoppage (used when canal is closed for repairs)
clé (f)	spanner
clé à molette	adjustable spanner
clin (m)	clinker
construit à clin	clinker-built
cloison (f)	bulkhead
cloison étanché	watertight bulkhead
clou (m)	nail
confluent	confluence (of rivers)
contre-plaqué (m)	plywood
cordage (m)	rope
croisement (m)	meeting (two boats)
cylindre (m)	cylinder
dalot (m)	scupper
dames de uage	rowlocks
darse (f)	tidal basin, dock
démarrer	to unmoor

Glossary of Words

French–English

démarreur (m)	starter (motor)
dépasser, trématter	to overtake
désarmer	to lay up (vessel)
digue (f)	dike, embankment, training wall
distributeur	distributor
distributeur de courant	distributor head
drisse (f)	halliard
drapeau (m)	flag
dynamo	dynamo
eau potable	drinking water
échelle (f)	ladder
écluse (f)	lock
éclusier	lock-keeper
écrou	nut
élinguer	to sling
épi (m)	training wall (river)
épicerie (f)	grocer
épisser	to splice
épissoir (m)	fid, marline-spike
épissure (f)	splice
une épissure à oeil	an eye-splice
épuisette (f)	bailer
équiper	to fit out (a boat)
écope (f)	bailer
essence (f)	petrol
extincteure (m)	fire extinguisher
faire le plein	fill up
fanal (m)	mast-head light
faubert	mop
feu (m)	light
feu-de-position	riding light
feux-de-route	navigation lights
fil (m)	wire, twine
fil de bougie	ignition wire
fil de caret	rope yarn
fil de cuivre rouge	copper wire
fil de fer	iron wire
fil de laiton	brass wire
fil de voile	sail twine
filtre (f)	filter
fond (m)	bottom
fraiser	to ream out, to countersink
fuel	diesel oil

119

French–English

fuite d'eau	leak
gaffe (f)	boathook
gasoil/mazout/fuel	diesel oil
gilet de sauvetage	lifejacket
gite	list, heel (of a boat)
goudron (m)	tar
goupille (f)	pin
goupille fendue	split-pin
gouvernail (m)	rudder
grau (m)	channel (connecting a salt lake with the sea)
guidon (m)	burgee, pennant
halage (m)	towage
chemin de halage	towpath
hausse (f)	rising water (river)
haut-fonds (m), bas-fonds	shallows, shoals
hélice	propeller
pas de l'hélice	pitch of propeller
hermétic (m)	jointing compound
hiloire (f)	a coaming
homme grenouille (m)	frogman
huile (f)	oil
injecteur (m)	injector
interrupteur (m)	switch (electric)
laiton (m)	brass
lampant	paraffin
largeur (f)	beam, breadth of beam
levier (m) (du rupteur)	contact-breaker arm
liège (m)	cork
lisse (f)	stringer, moulding, rubbing strake
magasin pour articles de la marine	ship's chandler
manchon (m)	collar, bush
manille (f)	shackle
manivelle (f)	lock-sluice handle
marcher en arrière, machine arrière	go astern
marin (m)	sailor (at sea)
marinier	sailor (inland), bargee
marteau (m)	hammer

mascaret (m)	bore, tidal wave
mazout/gasoil/fuel	diesel oil
mèche (f)	drill, bit, heart (of a rope)
menagiste	hardware
minium (m)	red lead
montant (m)/chandelier	stanchion
moteur	engine
moteur à quatre temps	four-stroke motor
moteur hors-bord	outboard engine
mouillage (m)	anchorage
mouiller	anchor, moor
niveau d'huile	oil level
noeud (m)	knot, bend, hitch
noeud d'arret	figure-of-eight
noeud de vache	granny knot
noeud d'anguille	running bowline
noeud de chaise	bowline
noeud plat	reef knot
noeude de grapplin	fisherman's bend
noeud d'écoute	sheet bend
demi-clef	half-hitch
deux demi-clefs à capeler	clove hitch
noeud de fouet	rolling hitch
noeud de bois	timber hitch
gueule de loup	Blackwall hitch
nouer	to hitch
ordre (m) d'allumage	firing order (motor)
palier (m)	bearing (machine)
palier à billes	ball-bearing
palier de butée	thrust bearing
papillon (m)	wing nut
pas (m)	pitch (of a screw or propeller)
passage rétrécis	narrow passage
passoire (f)	strainer, filter
patte (f) d'une ancre	flukes of an anchor
pattes d'araignée	oil grooves
pêcher	to fish
pêcheur	fisherman
péniche (f)	a barge
permit de circulation	cruising permit
pétrole (superieur) (m)	paraffin
pharmacien (m)	chemist

pilote (m)	pilot
pin (m)	pine
pitch-pin	pitchpine
pine (f)	pliers
piquet (m)	picket, stake
piston (m)	piston
plat-bord	gunwale
plot (m)	contact-point (motor)
poinçon (m)	pricker, bradawl
pointeau (m)	centre-punch, needle of carburettor
pomme (f)	truck (of a mast)
pompe (f)	pump
pompe de cale	bilge-pump
allumer une pompe	prime a pump
pompe de circulation	circulatory pump
pompe en essence	petrol pump
pont-canal (m)	aqueduct
poulie (f)	sheave
poulie coupée	snatch block
poulie double	double block
poulie simple	single block
prélart (m)	tarpaulin
presse-étoupe (m)	stuffing box or gland
quincaillerie (f)	ironmongery
râblure (f)	rabbet
rabot (m)	plane
passer le robot sur	to plane
radeau (m)	raft
radiateur (m)	radiator
rame (f)	file, oar
ras (m) de marée	tidal wave
recharge de gaz	gas refills
reducteur	reduction gear
remous (m)	wash (of a boat)
reniveler la batterie	top-up battery
réservoir à eau	water tank
réservoir d'essence/gas oil	fuel tank
rive droite	right bank
rive gauche	left bank
robinet (m)	tap
rondelle (f)	washer
sapin (m)	fir, deal, spruce

French–English

sas (m)	lock chamber
sasser	lock through
scaphandrier (m)	diver
signal sonrore	horn
ski nautique	water ski
souder	weld, solder
souder à l'autogene	oxyacetelyne, weld
souder à l'étain	soft solder
soupape	valve
souterrain (m)	tunnel
surbau (m)	coaming
surlier	whip (a rope)
surlieure (f)	whipping (of a rope)
taquet (m)	cleat, kevel
tarière (f)	auger
tirant d'eau (m)	draught (of ship)
tirant d'air	air draught
tornon (m)	strand (of a rope)
toueur (m)	tow-boat (operated by a chain in the river bed)
tour (m)	turn
un tour mort	a round turn
tournevisse	screwdriver
trématage (m)	overtaking (canal)
tribord	starboard
tuyau flexible (m)	hose
vadrouille	mop
valve, valvule (f)	valve
vanne (f)	sluice
vanne de prise d'eau	watercock
versant (m)	watershed
vilebrequin (m)	brace
vilebrequin à cliquet	ratchet-brace
virement (m)	turning, turn
virer	to turn (a boat)
vis (f)	screw
serrer vis	screw up
dévisser, déserrer	unscrew
visser	to screw
voie (f) d'eau	leak
faire une voie d'eau	spring a leak
aveugler une voie d'eau	stop a leak

123

Business Hours for Lock-keepers; Speed Limits; Public Holidays

BUSINESS HOURS FOR LOCK-KEEPERS

1 October to 30 November	0700–1800
1 December to 31 January	0730–1730
February	0700–1800
March	0700–1900
1 April to 30 September	0630–1930

On the Seine, from Port à l'Anglais to Cléon, the locks function all the year from 0700–1900. On the Rhône, downstream of Lyon, the locks are operational all the year between 0500–2100. All locks shut on Easter Day, 1 May, 14 July, 11 November, 25 December.

SPEED LIMITS

In principle they are as follows, but may be changed without notice if circumstances require:

Rivers:	generally	10kph (6mph)
Canals:	generally	6kph (3·7mph)
Brittany Canals		5kph (3mph)
Rhône		25kph (15·5mph)
Lower Seine (upstream)		15kph (9mph)
Lower Seine (downstream)		18kph (11mph)

PUBLIC HOLIDAYS

1 January, Easter Monday, 1 May, Ascension Day, Whit Monday, 14 July, 15 August, 1 November, 11 November, Christmas Day.

Page 125 (above) The quay below the *Institut*—Paris; (below) leaving the Cité—Notre Dame, Paris

Page 126 (*above*) Summer afternoons on the banks of the Seille; (*below*) reflections in the Yonne

Useful Addresses

Bureau des Transports Exceptionels,
162 rue du Faubourg St Martin,
75 Paris 10.

French Railways Limited, Touring Club of France,
French Tourist Office—all at:
178 Piccadilly,
London W1.

Touring Club de France,
65 Avenue de la Grande Armée,
75 Paris.

Ministère de l'Equipement et du Logement,
Direction des Ports Maritimes et des Voies Navigables,
Voies Navigables,
2e Bureau,
244 Boulevard St-German,
75 Paris 7.

Bureau des Douanes pour le Tourism,
182 rue St-Honoré,
75 Paris.

L'Office National de la Navigation,
2 Boulevard de Latour-Maubourg,
75 Paris 7.

Automobile Association,
Fanum House,
Leicester Square,
London WC2.

NAMES OF JOURNALS WITH INFORMATION ON INLAND WATER-
WAYS SUITABLE FOR BOATS

Practical Boat Owner (monthly)
Motor Boat and Yachting (fortnightly)
Yachting & Boating Weekly (weekly)
Small Boat and Light Craft (monthly)

Cruise Operators

In addition to those services listed below, there are a number of 'vedette' services—small passenger boats making local cruises through the towns in which they are to be found. There are several in Paris and others are to be encountered in 'river' towns like Rouen, Lyon, etc. There are no longer any cruise services operating on the French Meuse or the Doubs. There are some cruise possibilities on the Lac du Bourget and the Lac d'Annecy as well as from the French shore of Lake Geneva. Many of these services are subject to constant alteration both in the scope of their operations and the prices charged. You should, therefore, check with the operators or local tourist offices to keep abreast of the possibilities each year.

For those interested in hiring craft for *local* sailing, rowing or canoeing there is an excellent pamphlet, 'Yachting in France', obtainable free from the French Tourist Office in London (see Appendix B for address).

Name Owner or Agent	Port	Local cruise area	Type of boat(s)	Equipment	Price of boat per week	Literature in English	Season	Remarks
Holland-River Line, Wijnhaven 74, Rotterdam, Holland	Rotterdam	Rhine	Passenger boat (215 capacity)	Cabins, restaurant, services	£40–£100 per cruise	No	May to Oct	3–7 day cruises include the French Rhine
Cie de Navigation Mixte, 3 rue Président Carnot, Lyon 2, France	Lyon	Rhône	Passenger boat (250 capacity)	Restaurant bar, shop, swimming-pool	approx £35	No	April to Oct	3 day cruises, Lyon to Arles. Accommodation in intermediate ports included in price
Blue-Line Cruisers Limited, Le Grand Bassin, 11 Castelnaudary, France	Castelnaudary (Canal du Midi)	Canal du Midi, Canal Latéral à la Garonne	2–8 berth cabin cruisers	Fully equipped but linen and towels charged extra	£40–£170	Yes	All year	'Excursion' air fares to Toulouse available. Turn-round base at Marseillan (Etang du Thau)
Armement Lebert-Buisson, 24 Quai de Versailles, Nantes 44, France	Nantes	Erdre	Passenger boat (Vedette)	—	£1.20	No	Summer	
Dolphin Cruise Lines Limited, 2/5 Old Bond Street, London W1	Paris	Seine, Yonne, Marne	Passenger boat (converted barge) (34 capacity)	Cabins, restaurant, bar	£75–£105	Yes	May to Oct	Fortnightly cruises
Cornelder's Travel, Baltic House, 27 Leadenhall Street, London EC3	Amsterdam	Rhine	Passenger boat (140 capacity)	Cabins, restaurant, bar	approx £80	Yes	April to Oct	8 and 15 day cruises include the French Rhine. Cost includes travel London/Amsterdam

Company	Base port	Waterways	Boat	Facilities	Price		Season	Notes
Continental Waterway Cruises Ltd 22 Hans Place, London SW1	(No base port)	Burgundy waterways	Passenger boat (converted barge) (18 capacity)	Cabins, restaurant, bar	£82–£115	Yes	April to Oct	Circular tour in stages of 7 days
Continental Waterway Cruises Ltd 22 Hans Place, London SW1	Marseillan	Canal du Midi	Passenger boat (converted barge) (12 capacity)	Cabins, restaurant, bar	£74–£98 (inc breakfast & lunch)	Yes	April to Nov	Cruising alternate fortnights, Castelnaudary–Béziers–Aigues Mortes, connecting service Toulouse and Montpellier airports
Locazur, 24 rue St Martin, Paris 4	Golfe Juan, Antibes	Côte d'Azur, Canal du Midi	4 and 6 berth motor sailers 4 berth motor boats 6 berth motor sailers	Fully equipped	£60–£325	Yes	All year	Motor sailers need masts stepping for inland cruising
Régie Départementale des Passages d'Eau, BP 12, La Rochelle-Pallice 17, France	Rochefort	Charente river upstream to Cognac	Passenger boat (150 capacity)	Restaurant, bar, no cabins	60p–£1.50 per day cruise	Yes	May to Sept	Adequate accommodation at terminus ports
Société Caravaneau, 2 rue du Moussel, 27–Vernon, France	Vernon	Seine, Oise	Floating caravans (self-propelled) 2–6 berth	Without linen	£70–£170	No	All year	—
Panalpina Travel, 12A Well Court, Bow Lane, London EC4	Rhine ports	Rhine, Lower Mosel	Passenger boats (130 and 150 capacity)	Cabins, restaurant, services	£30–£167 per cruise	Yes	April to Sept	Cruises of 4–16 days (only the longer cruises take in the French Rhine)

Name	Port	Local cruise area	Type of boat(s)	Equipment	Price of boat per week	Literature in English	Season	Remarks
Loc Armor, Armor Marine, Quai Garnier du Fougeray, 35 – St Malo, France	St Malo, Dinan, Redon	Breton waterways and coastal	Motor sailers, sailing dinghies, floating caravans (self-propelled, 4 berth)	Without linen	£15–£65	Yes	All year	One-way journeys (with free transfer of your car between ports if desired)
Marin 'Air, 11 Salleles d'Aude, France	Salleles d'Aude (*Canal du Midi*)	*Canal de Jonction, Canal de la Robine, Canal du Midi*, coastal	4–8 berth cabin cruisers, floating caravans (self-propelled, 4 berth)	Fully equipped but linen and towels charged extra	£50–£180	Yes	All year	
Natour SA, Peniche West Navigation 78 – Port Marly, France	Port Marly, Peronne, Auxerre	Seine, Somme, Nivernais	4–6 berth cabin cruisers, floating caravans (self-propelled, 4 berth)	Without linen	£38–£265	No	All year	English agents: Boat Enquiries Limited, 12 Western Road, Oxford
PGL Adventure Limited, Station Street, Ross-on-Wye, Herefordshire	—	Ardèche river	Canoe		£56	Yes	June to Sept	15 day coach tour to Mediterranean including descent of Ardeche by canoe
Tourisme Nautique Breton, 29 Avenue Roosevelt, 56 – Vannes, France	Redon	Breton waterways	3–8 berth cabin cruisers, floating caravans (self-propelled, 5 berth)	Without linen	£50–£160	No	All year	

Company	Location / River	Boat type	Equipment	Price	English	Season	Notes
Saint Line Cruisers, La Montagne, La Collancelle, 58 – Corbigny, France	La Collancelle *Canal du Nivernais*, (*Canal du Nivernais*), Poincy (River Marne) *Canal du Bourgogne*, Yonne, *Canal de Bourgogne*, Marne	4/6 berth cabin cruisers	Fully equipped but linen charged extra	£61-£146	Yes	March to Nov	Correspondence in English. A turn-round base (for one-way cruises) at Pouilly-en-Auxois (*Canal du Bourgogne*)
L'Hotel de la Marine, Caudebec-en-Caux, 76, France	Caudebec (Villequier-Jumieges) Seine	Passenger boat (Vedette)	—	40p-£1.10 per cruise	No	Easter to Sept	—
M Couly, 9 rue Fourrier, 30 – Beaucaire France	Beaucaire Rhône	Passenger boat (35 capacity)	Light refreshments (no alcohol)	£5 per 2 day cruise	No	April to Sept	Other cruises also available. Check with company
Société Général de Touage et de Remorquage, 5 quai Malaquais, 75 – Paris XI	Carennac Dordogne	'Gabarre' (open flat-bottomed boat) (14 capacity)	—	£72 approx per cruise	Yes	June to Sept	6-day cruise Carennac to Beynac. Descent of river by stages. Accommodation ashore

Inland Waterways Local Authorities

Town	Departments covered	Addresses
Lille	Nord Pas-de-Calais	Service de la Navigation, 37 rue du Plat, 59 – Lille. Telephone: 57–16–24
Compiègne	Somme Oise Aisne Marne	Service de la Navigation, 2 boulevard Gambetta 60 – Compiègne. Telephone: 440–15–80
Charleville	Ardennes Meuse	Direction Départementale de l'Equipement, 13 place Winston-Churchill, 08 – Charleville. Telephone: 32–29–35
Nancy	Moselle Meurthe-et-Moselle Vosges Haute-Marne	Service de la Navigation, 28 boulevard Albert-ler, 54 – Nancy, Telephone: 53–60–24
Strasbourg	Bas-Rhin Haut-Rhin Territoire-de-Belfort	Service de la Navigation, 25 rue de la Nuée-Bleue, 67 – Strasbourg. Telephone: 32–36–15
Rouen	Seine-Maritime Eure Manche Calvados Orne Eure-et-Loir	Service de la Navigation, (Direction du Port Autonome), 52 quai Gaston-Boulet, 76 – Rouen. Telephone: 71–74–54
Paris	Paris Hauts-de-Seine Seine-St-Denis Val-de-Marne Yvelines Essonne	Service de la Navigation, 2 quai de Grenelle, 75 Paris XVe, Telephone: 577–32–92

Town	Departments covered	Addresses
	Val-d'Oise	
	Seine-et-Marne	
	Aube	
	Yonne	
Dijon	Côte d'Or	Direction Départementale de l'Equipement, 57 rue de Mulhouse, 21 – Dijon. Telephone: 32–35–06
Nevers	Loiret	Direction Départementale de l'Equipement,
	Nièvre	l'Equipement,
	Allier	2 rue de la Poissonnerie,
	Loire	58 – Nevers.
	Haute-Loire	Telephone: 61–11–43
	Puy-de-Dôme	
Bourges	Loir-et-Cher	Direction Départementale de l'Equipement,
	Indre-et-Loire	l'Equipement,
	Indre	Centre Administratif Condé,
	Cher	18 – Bourges.
	Vienne	Telephone: 24–40–27
	Haute-Vienne	
	Creuse	
Nantes	Finistère	Service de la Navigation,
	Côtes-du-Nord	(Direction du Port Autonome)
	Morbihan	2 place de l'Edit-de-Nantes,
	Ille-et-Vilaine	44 – Nantes.
	Mayenne	Telephone: 71–37–20
	Sarthe	
	Loire-Atlantique	
	Maine-et-Loire	
	Vendée	
	Deux-Sèvres	
Bordeaux	Charente-Maritime	Service de la Navigation,
	Charente	(Direction du Port Autonome)
	Gironde	Palais de la Bourse,
	Dordogne	Place Gabriel,
	Corrèze	33 – Bordeaux.
	Landes	Telephone: 52–60–61
	Pyrénées-Atlantiques	
Toulouse	Cantal	Service de la Navigation,
	Lot	2 port St-Etienne,
	Aveyron	31 – Toulouse.
	Lozère	Telephone: 80–79–91
	Lot-et-Garonne	
	Tarn-et-Garonne	

Town	*Departments covered*	*Addresses*
	Tarn	
	Gers	
	Hautes-Pyrénées	
	Haute-Garonne	
	Ariège	
	Aude	
	Pyrénées-Orientales	
Lyon	Haute-Saône	Service de la Navigation,
	Doubs	2 quai de la Quarantaine,
	Jura	69 – Lyon.
	Saône-et-Loire	Telephone: 42–55–83
	Rhône	
	Ain	
	Haute-Savoie	
	Isère	
	Ardèche	
	Drôme	
	Hautes-Alpes	
	Basses-Alpes	
	Vaucluse	
	Gard	
	Hérault	
	Bouches-du-Rhône	
	Var	
	Alpes-Maritimes	
Ajaccio	Corse	Direction Départementale de
		l'Equipement,
		13 rue Maréchal-Ornano,
		20 – Ajaccio.
		Telephone: 002–955

Waterways Synopsis

This Appendix lists most of the navigable rivers and canals shown on the map at the rear of the book, except those in the very north-east corner of France which are unlikely to be of great interest to the visitor.

Of the four unqualified metric dimensions shown, the first two refer to the lock dimensions (length and width), the third to the normal minimum depth of the waterway (if this dimension is often subject to reduction—for instance, during drought—the temporary minimum is given in brackets); and the last refers to the minimum bridge heights.

Adour (river)
66km, no locks. Mainly tidal. Bridges: 6m50. Attractive Basque scenery. Almost no traffic. Dangerous below Bayonne.

Aisne (canalised river)
57km, 7 locks. 46m00 × 7m95 × 2m10, 3m70. Some surprisingly attractive stretches though often close to main road and railway. Quite busy.

Aisne (lateral canal)
51km, 8 locks. 38m50 × 5m20 × 2m20, 3m40. Comments as above.

Aisne à Marne (canal)
58km, 24 locks. 38m50 × 5m20 × 2m20, 3m48. Not par-

ticularly attractive open, undulating country. Considerable traffic to Reims.

Ardennes (canal)
  88km, 44 locks. 38m50×5m20×2m00, 3m70. Pleasant wooded scenery; hilly. Moderate traffic.

Arles à Bouc (canal)
  47km, 4 locks. 33m00×8m00×2m00 (1m60), 3m50. Flat, marshy 'Van Gogh' country. Almost no traffic.

Blavet (canalised river)
  60km, 28 locks. 26m30×4m70×1m60, 2m00. An attractive river meandering through peaceful countryside.

Bourgogne or *Burgundy* (canal)
  242km, 190 locks. 39m00×5m20×2m20, 3m40. Beautiful pastoral landscape; spectacular wooded cliffs west of Dijon. Uninteresting then dull to Saône. Almost no traffic.

Briare (canal)
  54km, 32 locks. 39m00×5m20×1m60, 3m50. Gently undulating. Woods, lakes and open country. First large European canal with summit level, completed 1642. Terminates with spectacular aqueduct over Loire. Moderate traffic.

Centre (canal)
  112km, 61 locks. 39m00×5m20×2m00, 3m70. Pleasant varied scenery but industrialised around Montceau. Moderate traffic.

Charente (canalised river)
  120km, 20 locks. Only the first 3 locks are officially maintained. The rest of the locks on this beautiful river (which passes through many places of interest) can usually be worked after local enquiry and with local co-operation. Depth variable but 3ft usually obtainable. Considerable weed.

Dordogne (river)
117km, no locks. Mostly tidal. Depth 1m25 below Branne (0m30 above Branne). Bridges: 5m90. Subject to drought. Not the most interesting part of a beautiful river.

Erdre (river)
6km, no locks. Depth: 2m00, no bridges. The 'Bosphorus' of France—the river forms a narrow lake with wooded sides. Much sailing.

Est (canal)
Northern section: Belgian border to Marne au Rhin canal
272km, 59 locks. 38m50×5m20×2m20, 3m70. Pleasant pastoral scenery. Meuse valley. Light traffic.

Est (canal)
Southern section: Marne au Rhin canal to Saône
147km, 99 locks. 38m50×5m13×2m20, 3m70. Follows Moselle valley, then crosses foothills of Vosges. Beautiful and largely deserted.

Garonne (canalised river)
Navigable for 61km from Bordeaux. No locks. Depth: 1m10, bridges: 6m50. (After Bordeaux dangerous for inland craft.) Tidal; vineyards, châteaux and pine trees. Very little traffic. Subject to irregular tidal bore.

Garonne (lateral canal)
193km, 53 locks. 30m65×6m00×2m00, 3m60. Very attractive 'mixed' scenery toward west, much less good near Toulouse. Light traffic. (Branch to Montauban: 11km, 10 locks.)

Ille-et-Rance (canal)
85km, 48 locks. 27m10×4m70×1m60, 2m30. Crosses a quiet and beautiful part of Brittany. Very little traffic.

Loing (canal)
   49km, 20 locks. 39m10×5m20×2m20, 3m70. Pleasant, fairly wooded and flat. Moderate traffic.

Loire (river)
   From Nantes to junction with Maine: 85km, no locks. Depth: 1m50 (0m35); bridges: 6m50. Interesting places and scenery. Below Nantes is not suitable for inland craft. No official navigation upstream of junction with Maine, therefore at navigator's risk. But Saumur is usually possible and Tours may be reached under favourable conditions. Sandbanks, draglines and underwater obstacles present formidable risks.

Loire (lateral canal)
   196km, 37 locks. 39m00×5m12×2m20, 3m70. Quiet, pleasant and very flat scenery and many interesting places. Moderate traffic.

Marne (canalised river)
   178km, 18 locks. 45m00×7m80×2m20, 3m80. The upstream end is the most attractive. Passes through the Champagne area. Can be difficult in times of flood. Moderate traffic.

Marne (lateral canal)
   67km, 15 locks. 38m50×5m20×2m20, 3m70. Not of great scenic interest but pleasant, if flattish. Light traffic.

Marne au Rhin (canal)
   313km, 160 locks. 38m70×5m13×2m20, 3m70. Not especially attractive except towards eastern end (over Vosges). But plenty to interest the canal enthusiast, including 5 tunnels and a major inclined plane at Arzviller. Fairly busy.

Marne à la Saône (canal)
   224km, 114 locks. 38m30×5m10×2m20, 3m51. Attractive scenery all the way. Light traffic.

Mayenne—Maine (river)
135km, 45 locks. 31m00 × 5m20 × 1m50, 3m50. Beautiful valley for whole length. No traffic. Threatened with closure.

Meuse (river)
See Canal de l'Est.

Midi (canal)
240km, 101 locks. 30m00 × 5m50 × 1m80, 3m50 (bridges steeply arched). One of the best known canals of Europe, opened 1681 and largely in original state. 'Contour' canal often above valley floor. Views to Pyrenees, open country; vines, fruit, cypresses. Attractive for whole length. Includes famous 7 lock staircase and aqueduct at Béziers. Much to interest tourists at Carcassonne. Very light commercial traffic but an increasing volume of pleasure craft.

Moselle (canalised river)
This river is in the course of being opened to large-scale traffic and the 14 locks are being reduced to 4. The French Moselle is not very attractive to visitors.

Nantes à Brest (canal)
227km, 119 locks, not including section from Guerlédan to Brest which is closed. 25m70 × 4m65 × 1m60 (1m30), 3m15. Offers a beautiful and peaceful journey across Southern Brittany. Very little traffic.

Nivernais (canal)
174km, 114 locks. 30m15 × 5m10 × 1m60, 2m71. Part canal, part river. Across beautiful hilly countryside. Includes 3 tunnels and a river crossing. Almost deserted by commercial traffic but increasingly popular to pleasure craft.

Oise (river)
104km, 7 locks. 41m00 × 6m00 × 2m50, 6m05 (4m10). A

once beautiful valley now industrialised in many places but some attractive stretches remaining. Fairly busy.

Oise (lateral canal)

34km, 4 locks. 39m00×6m00×2m60, 4m10. Not unattractive but busy.

Oise à l'Aisne (canal)

48km, 13 locks. 40m50×6m00×2m60, 3m70. An attractive canal passing quiet, flattish and wooded scenery. One long tunnel. Quite busy.

Oudon (canalised river)

18km, 3 locks. 33m00×5m20×1m70 (1m00), 3m60. Beautiful river, entirely deserted and threatened with closure.

Rhône (river)

282km, 12 locks (some in course of construction). Depth: 1m50 (1m10); bridges: 6m30. Spectacular scenery, several gorges, many interesting places. Vast engineering schemes. Construction of all works not yet complete and several stretches are still very dangerous due to rapid current and rocky bottom. Pilotage (obtainable from Port de Plaisance office in Lyon) essential. Approximately £35 for two-day journey. For return journey, tow (£100 approximately) is required for boats unable to maintain at least 10 knots.

Rhône au Rhin (canal)

320km, 163 locks. 38m70×5m10×2m20, 3m55. Passes through beautiful hilly country between the Vosges and Jura mountains. Main road and railway are seldom too near to be a nuisance. Light traffic.

Rhône à Sète (canal)

98km, 2 locks. 80m00×12m00×2m00, 4m32. Interesting for its passage through north of Camargue. Very flat marsh-

Page 143 (*above*) Barging the old way; (*below*) fishing port of Mèze on the Etang de Thau

Page 144 (*left*) Fin de siècle—exuberance in a summer villa on the Marne; (*above right*) a typical canal aqueduct; (*below right*) haulage rope chafing on a bridge abutment

land with much to fascinate the naturalist. Beware of mosquitoes in late summer.

Roanne à Digoin (canal)
 55km, 10 locks. 39m00 × 5m20 × 2m20, 3m70. A pastoral flat canal cut which is totally peaceful and seldom passes even a village. Almost deserted.

Sambre (river)
 52km, 9 locks. 38m50 × 5m20 × 2m30, 3m28. Some industry but surprisingly attractive on the whole. Fairly busy.

Sambre à l'Oise (canal)
 67km, 38 locks. 37m60 × 5m15 × 2m20, 3m70. Comments as above.

Saône (river)
Upper section: Corre to St-Symphorien
 158km, 19 locks. 38m50 × 5m20 × 2m10, 3m52. Very beautiful river, flowing slowly and cleanly between low hills. Two tunnels. Very little traffic.
Lower section: St-Symphorien to Lyon
 217km, 11 locks. 39m50 × 8m00 × 2m00, 3m50. A wide river flowing through a somewhat featureless plain. Some interesting towns. Moderate traffic.

Sarthe (river)
 131km, 20 locks. 30m85 × 5m15 × 1m40 (1m00), 3m40. Beautiful valley. No traffic. Threatened with closure.

Seille (river)
 39km, 4 locks. 35m60 × 5m17 × 1m50, 4m70. Very beautiful and completely peaceful. One commercial craft left. Threatened with closure.

Seine (river)
 Upper section: upstream limit to Montereau

67km, 13 locks. 38m90×7m90×1m70, 4m23. Attractive, undulating and fairly open country. Very light traffic.

Middle section: Montereau to Paris

104km, 11 locks. 172m00×11m80×2m00, 6m00 (3m50). Except in the Forest of Fontainebleau, not particularly attractive and substantial industry. Fairly heavy traffic.

Lower section: Paris to Rouen

242km, 7 locks. 151m25×11m80×2m20, 6m00 (3m50). Once beautiful valley, now almost ruined by industry and pollution. Very heavy traffic. Navigation through Paris is not for the beginner—detailed map essential. Last 40km downstream are tidal. (Rouen to Le Havre—126km—is considered as Marine Navigation.)

Sèvre-Nantaise (river)

22km, 1 lock, only open at high water. 32m00×5m60×2m30 (0m50), 4m00. A short but very lovely river. No traffic.

Sèvre-Niortaise (river)

54km, 8 locks. 31m50×5m20×1m20 (0m80). Has several short branch canals. Flows through a strange marshy area which is a network of fields and dykes.

Somme (canalised river)

156km, 25 locks. 38m50×6m35×1m80, 3m43. An attractive river flowing through a shallow valley of marshes and alders covered in mistletoe. Light traffic.

Thau (salt lake)

Length: 17½km; depth: 2m00, except near western shore. Delightful fishing ports around northern perimeter. Subject to sudden Mediterranean squalls which could endanger inland craft.

Vilaine (river)

95km, 14 locks. 19m40×4m40×0m90, 3m20. A peaceful and attractive river with very little traffic.

Yonne (river)

108km, 26 locks. 93m00×8m30×2m00, 4m40. Quite an attractive river though a little too near road and rail for complete peace. Fairly light traffic.

THROUGH ROUTE TO MEDITERRANEAN

The shortest route across France to the Mediterranean via Le Havre–Paris–Dijon–Lyon is approximately 1,300km and there are 249 locks. The alternative route via Nevers is 3km longer but there are 61 locks fewer.

Tunnels

The dimensions are given in the order: width, height and depth. These dimensions refer to the 'navigational rectangle'—the actual width and height usually being considerably in excess of these figures. The exceptions to this are marked * and on these tunnels the dimensions refer to the maximum width and the height to the apex of the vault.

Canal	Name	Dimensions	Length (metres)
Canal de l'Aisne à la Marne	Mont de Billy	5·10 × 3·70 2·50	2,300
Canal des Ardennes	St Aignan*	6·00 × 6·00 2·90	197
Canal de Bourgogne	Pouilly-en-Auxois	5·00 × 3·10 2·60	3,350
Canal de l'Est	Ham	5·80 × 3·60 2·20	565
Canal de l'Est	Revin	5·95 × 3·60 2·20	224
Canal de l'Est	Verdun	5·80 × 3·70 2·20	45
Canal de l'Est	Koeurs	5·80 × 3·70 2·20	50
Canal St-Maur (Marne)	St Maur	7·50 × 3·25 2·15	600
Canal de Meaux à Chalifert (Marne)	Chalifert	6·50 × 4·00 2·20	290
Canal de la Marne au Rhin	Mauverges	5·25 × 3·25 2·20	4,877
Canal de la Marne au Rhin	Foug	5·25 × 3·25 2·20	867
Canal de la Marne au Rhin	Liverdun	5·25 × 3·25 2·20	388
Canal de la Marne au Rhin	Niederviller	6·60 × 4·50 2·70	475
Canal de la Marne au Rhin	Arzviller	6·60 × 4·50 2·70	2,307

Tunnels

Canal	Name	Dimensions	Length (metres)
Canal de la Marne à la Saône	Balesmes	4·00 × 5·10 2·50	4,820
Canal de la Marne à la Saône	Condes	4·00 × 5·10 2·50	308
Canal de Marseille au Rhône	Rove (temporarily closed)	22·00 × 11·40 4·00	7,120
Canal de Midi	Malpas*	5·70 × 6·40 2·00	161
Canal du Nivernais	Collancelle	5·60 × 3·75 1·60	758
Canal du Nivernais	Mouas	5·60 × 3·75 1·60	268
Canal du Nivernais	Breuilles	5·60 × 3·75 1·60	212
Canal de l'Oise à l'Aisne	Braye-en-Laonnois	6·50 × 3·50 3·60	2,365
Canal de Rhône au Rhin	Thoraise	5·50 × 4·10 2·50	185
Canal de Rhône au Rhin	Tarragnoz	5·50 × 4·10 2·50	394
Canal de St-Quentin	Bony	5·00 × 3·58 2·80	5,670
Canal de St-Quentin	Lesdins	5·00 × 3·58 2·80	1,098
River Saône	St Albin*	6·55 × 4·10 2·00	681
River Saône	Seveux-Savoyeux	6·50 × 3·60 2·00	643

149

Addresses of Customs

The French Government has recently established a wide distribution of Customs Offices throughout the country. There are already 160 such offices in various parts of France, as well as at the frontiers.

Listed below are the main Regional Offices, together with their addresses and telephone numbers. These offices may be able to advise you of branch offices more convenient to you.

Paris: 14 rue Y-Toudic, 10e. Téléphone: 208-42-50 à 55.

Paris-Est: 16 rue Y-Toudic, 10e. Téléphone: 208-42-50.

Paris-Sud: 50 rue Louise-Chenu, 94 Limeil-Brevannes. Téléphone: 925-65-30. BP: 21 à Boissy-St-Léger 94.

Paris-Ouest: 5 rue Volta, 78 St-Germain-en-Laye. Téléphone: 963-33-00.

Dunkerque (59): 2 rue de Paris, BP 531. Téléphone: 66-78-16.

Lille (59): 93 boulevard Carnot. Téléphone: 55-23-02.

Valenciennes (59): 41 boulevard Watteau. Téléphone: 46-24-16 et 46-20-11.

Amiens (80): 6 rue des Lombards, BP 332. Téléphone: 91-82-57.

Reims (51): 110 rue du Jard, BP 382. Téléphone: 47-91-25.

Nancy (54): Terre-plein St-Epvre, BP 61. Téléphone: 52-05-90.

Metz (57): 25 avenue Foch, BP 1074. Téléphone: 68-75-85.

Strasbourg (67): 11 avenue de la Liberté, BP 1004 RP. Téléphone: 35-46-08.

Mulhouse (68): 13 rue du Tilleul, BP 3028. Téléphone: 45-86-19.

Besançon (25): 8 rue de la Préfecture. Téléphone: 83-71-71.

Dijon (21): 25 boulevard Voltaire, BP 1508. Téléphone: 32-58-17.

Lyon (69): 12 rue de l'Abbaye-d'Ainay (2e). Téléphone: 37-34-59 et 42-44-73.

Clermont-Ferrand (63): 8 rue de Rabanesse, BP 15. Téléphone: 93-83-93.

Chambéry (73): 1 rue Waldeck-Rousseau, BP 45. Téléphone: 34-02-20.

Nice (06): 10 avenue du Maréchal-Foch. Téléphone: 85-64-24.

Ajaccio (20): 3 parc Cunéo-d'Ornano, BP 86. Téléphone: 21-06-63 et 21-16-47.

Marseille (Provence) (13): 134 boulevard Michelet (8e). Téléphone: 76-37-43.

Marseille (13): 48 avenue R-Schumann (2e). Téléphone: 20-19-84 à 87.

Montpellier (34): 1 rue Cité Benoit. Téléphone: 92-79-18.

Perpignan (66): 7 avenue Pierre-Cambres, BP 947. Téléphone: 34-85-42.

Toulouse (31): 55 Grande-Rue St-Michel. Téléphone: 52-41-01.

Bayonne (64): 27 rue Lormand, BP 2. Téléphone: 25-06-54 et 25-29-72.

Bordeaux (33): 1 quai de la Douane, BP 903 RP. Téléphone: 44-47-10 et 08-43-36.

Poitiers (86): 10 rue Boncenne, BP 188. Téléphone: 41-46-26 et 41-59-79.

Orléans (45): 10 boulevard de Verdun, BP 711. Téléphone: 87-00-02.

Nantes (44): 7 place Mellinet, BP 1030. Téléphone: 73-80-70 (Loire).

Rennes (35): 21 boulevard du Colombier. CEDEX n° 2010 (35-Rennes-gare). Téléphone: 30-95-88 RENNE 73.048.

Caen (14): 44 quai Vendeuvre, BP 3101. Téléphone: 81-11-50.

Rouen (76): 13 avenue Mt-Riboudet. Téléphone: 70-43-93 et 70-58-90.

Le Havre (76): 201 boulevard de Strasbourg, BP 27. Téléphone: 42-77-62.

Maps and Publications

The following are obtainable from:
Journal de la Navigation,
29 Boulevard Henri-IV,
75 Paris IV.

	Price (*francs*)
Large, detailed map of the canals of France, Belgium, the Netherlands and Western Germany (in 4 sheets)	45
Small map of the canals of France and Belgium	20
Map of the Marne (from its confluence at Epernay)	26
Map of the French Meuse	29
Map of the navigable waterways of the Midi	8
Regulations applicable to the Moselle	9.50
Map of the Canal du Nord, with the regulations	2
Map of the navigable waterways of the west	8
Map showing areas for water-skiing, sailing, etc	12.50
Map of the Rhine from Bâle to Lauterbourg	20
Guide for the waterways Rhine to Saône, via Canal de l'Alsace and the Doubs	27
Map and guide to the Rhône, from Lyon downstream	39
Guide to the Saône	39
Map of the Saône, from Lyon to St-Jean-de-Losne, 1963 edition	17
Map of the Saône (on a very large scale)	48
Map of the lower Seine, from Paris to the sea	29
Map of the upper Seine, from Paris to Montereau	21
Map of the Yonne, from Auxerre to Montereau	21
Telephone numbers of the principal locks	3.50

In addition, the following maps are available from:
> M Henri Vagnon,
> 25 rue Mistral,
> 69-Caluire.

Guide to the Rhône, from Lyon downstream (1/20.000e)
Guide to the Saône
Guide to the Rhine to Saône (French and German)

Also,
> La Librairie Girard & Barrère,
> 35 bis, rue Henri-Barbusse,
> 75 Paris 5(e)

produces a map of the rivers and canals of France and Belgium (110×120cm) scale 1/1.000.000e.

And
> The Touring Club of France,
> 65 avenue de la Grande-Armee,
> Paris

issues several nautical guides to the interior waterways of France, especially for pleasure-boat drivers.

Guides: Lower Seine, Upper Seine, Oise and Aisne, Marne, Canals of Brittany, Paris–Amsterdam, Paris–Mediterranean
Maps: Oise and Aisne

Finally, the
> Librairie Berger-Levrault,
> 5 rue Auguste-Comte,
> 75 Paris 6

published, in 1965, a *Guide de la Navigation Interieure*—a guide to the inland waterways of France. It costs 100 francs and is in two volumes:

154

Maps and Publications

Volume I   Characteristics of Canals
            Tables of distances
            Administrative organisation
Volume II Map of the network of French inland waterways.
            Scale: 1km to 1cm

For detailed strip maps of cruising waterways, see *Navigator's Guide to the French Inland Waterways*, to be published by David & Charles.

APPENDIX I

Weights and Measures

Litres	Gallons		Km	Miles
1 =	0·22		1 =	0·62
2 =	0·44		2 =	1·24
3 =	0·66		3 =	1·86
4 =	0·88		4 =	2·48
5 =	1·10		5 =	3·11
6 =	1·32		6 =	3·73
7 =	1·54		7 =	4·35
8 =	1·76		8 =	4·97
9 =	1·98		9 =	5·59
10 =	2·20		10 =	6·21
15 =	3·30		15 =	9·32
20 =	4·40		20 =	12·43
30 =	6·60		30 =	18·64
40 =	8·80		40 =	24·85
50 =	11·00		50 =	31·07
100 =	22·00		100 =	62·14

lb	kg
1 =	0·453
2 =	0·907
3 =	1·360
4 =	1·814
5 =	2·268
6 =	2·721
7 =	3·175
8 =	3·628
9 =	4·082
10 =	4·535